The Used Car Buyer's Manual

HOW TO FIND THE BEST BUY ON A USED CAR

DAVID J. BUECHEL

pyramid west publishing

Disclaimer

The purpose of this book is to educate and entertain. It is designed to provide information in regard to the subject matter covered. Every effort has been made to make this manual as complete and as accurate as possible. However, in the purchasing of a used car, there are problems, both observable and unobservable, that are too numerous to cover in a book. Therefore, the buyer assumes all risks and should always beware when purchasing a car. The author and Pyramid West Publishing shall have neither liability nor responsibility to any person or entity with respect to any loss or damage caused, or alleged to be caused, directly or indirectly by the information contained in this book. This manual should only be used as a general guide and not as the ultimate source for car buying.

Library of Congress Catalog Card Number: 95-70448

ISBN 0-9647780-0-9

Acknowledgments

First of all I would like to thank my Mother and my Father for teaching me some smarts. Thanks, Dad, for the expert illustrations, too. Not bad for an ex-sign painter. I would also like to thank Linda Jordan for her patience, understanding, and moral support and all the free photocopying; proofers Lori Lord, Allyson Martin, and Terri Nigro, who bailed me out of punctuation hell; and John Thomson who also made a contribution to this book.

TABLE OF CONTENTS

Introduction

PART I:
HOW TO BUY A USED CAR
FROM A PRIVATE PARTY

PART II:
HOW TO BUY A USED CAR
FROM A DEALER

Chapter 6: Dealing With Dealers   85

PART III:
HOW TO SELL AND CARE FOR YOUR USED CAR

Introduction

First of all I would like to thank you for purchasing this manual. You have just made a smart move, because this book is designed to save you time and money. And time and money will indeed be saved--I guarantee it.

As with any written information, you will benefit the most by studying and memorizing what is being presented to you here. All the chapters have been written in easy-to-understand English, and all the crucial information has been printed in capital letters, so DON'T FORGET WHAT IS WRITTEN IN CAPS!

The first part of *The Used Car Buyer's Manual* focuses on buying a used car from a private individual. I notice that all the other car buying guides currently on the market seem to miss the boat on this subject by usually only offering one small chapter. This is an area I emphasize because you benefit most by avoiding the dealers and negotiating with someone who is on the same level as you. The used car lots should be left as a last resort.

However, if you reach the point where you must buy through a dealer, you need not worry. I offer plenty of information in the second part of my book: *How to Buy a Used Car From a Dealer.* This is where I go into detail on everything from dealer shenanigans to, well, dealer shenanigans.

Unlike all the other car buying guides available, I offer a reliable used car directory in Appendix A which can save you time and legwork by immediately starting you off on the right foot. Everyone knows that not all cars are created equal. Instead of having to spend hours at the library reading up on automotive ratings to weed out the reliables from the undesirables, I have already done that for you. This creates a nice shortcut to making a smart used car investment.

As for the auto inspection, there's no need to take notes. I have already done that for you too. In Appendix B you will find a comprehensive inspection checklist which I welcome you to photocopy (for personal use, of course). It follows the steps in Chapters 3 and 4 almost verbatim, making it as convenient as possible for you to perform a thorough inspection.

As you can see, I tried my hardest to take the misery and the mystery out of buying a used car. But I didn't stop there. In the third and final part of *The Used Car Buyer's Manual,* I detail how to sell your car for the maximum amount of money, while offering advise and tips on car care.

I spent a year of my life writing this manual and the previous 16 years at the school of hard knocks learning it. Now the ball is your court. With a little time and effort on your part, you can learn in a week or two what took me many years (and much, much more $$$) to learn. Now, without further adieu, thanks again and good luck!

PART I:

HOW TO BUY A USED CAR FROM A PRIVATE PARTY

CHAPTER 1:

RESEARCH

THE GOOD, THE BAD, AND THE UGLY

Why research? Because research will reveal the good, the bad, and the ugly things we need to know about cars BEFORE we buy. You wouldn't want someone else's problems, would you? Start thinking of a used car in terms of an investment. After all, it IS an investment. You need dependable transportation to commute to work so you can make a living, right? A second-hand car that continuously breaks down, drains you of your hard-earned money, and depreciates radically would certainly be a bad investment.

However, a reliable auto that never needs anything beyond normal maintenance will depreciate gradually--making it a good investment. That's what this chapter (and the rest of the book) is all about, separating the good from the bad and the ugly.

The first part can all be done on paper, through research, long before you look at any cars for sale. That's the beauty of buying used. With little difficulty, you can find out which cars offer the best track record.

The second part is finding one of those dependable cars that has been well cared for by its past owner(s) and selling at fair market value. In order to capitalize on this kind of investment, you must do your homework. IT ALL BEGINS WITH RESEARCH!

Before we continue, I must assume that maybe you don't know a thing about cars. If so, just let me clarify. You will see the words *make* and *model* used frequently in the coming pages. Just so there isn't any confusion, *make* refers to the auto maker, like Ford, Chrysler, and Toyota, while *model* refers to the maker's product line, like Mustang, LeBaron, and Corolla, respectively.

Another term I use frequently is "bargaining leverage." What I mean by bargaining leverage is, say you looked at a car that was selling for $5,000 and discovered that the car needs new tires. You would then use the cost of new tires as a reason to lower the price. In other words, if new tires cost $300, then you would naturally expect to get the car for $4,700. You're using the worn tires as bargaining leverage.

USED CAR CLASSIFICATIONS

If you already know the type of car you want, fast forward to the **Best Used Car Bets** section on page 16 and seriously consider the cars from my personal picks list. However, if you are uncertain as to what type of car you want at this point, then you have a few more decisions to make. The following autos have been categorized by size and type to help you place yourself and narrow your focus. DO NOT CONFUSE THIS LIST WITH MY PERSONAL PICKS LIST.

Small Cars
Some examples are: Chevrolet Cavalier, Dodge Colt, Eagle Summit, Ford Escort and Festiva, Geo Metro and Prizm, Honda Civic, Hyundai Excel, Mercury Tracer, Nissan Sentra, Plymouth Sundance, Pontiac Sunbird, Subaru Justy, Toyota Corolla and Tercel, and Volkswagen Fox, Golf, and Jetta.

Mid-Size Cars
Some mid-size cars are Buick Century and Regal, Chevrolet Corsica and Lumina, Chrysler LeBaron, Dodge Dynasty, Ford Taurus and Thunderbird, Honda Accord, Mazda 626, Mercury Cougar and Sable, Mitsubishi Galant, Oldsmobile Cutlass Ciera and Cutlass Supreme, Plymouth Acclaim, Pontiac Grand Prix and Grand Am, Subaru Legacy, Toyota Camry, Volkswagon Passat, and Volvo 240.

Full-Size Cars
Some big American boats are Buick LeSabre, Chevrolet Caprice, Dodge Diplomat, Ford Crown Victoria, Mercury Grand Marquis, Oldsmobile Delta 88, and Pontiac Bonneville.

Luxury Cars
It's hard to find a crank-up window in one of these: BMW 850i, Buick Riviera, Chrysler Fifth Avenue, Nissan Maxima, Mazda 929, Oldsmobile 98, Saab 9000, and all models by Cadillac, Infiniti, Jaguar, Lexus, Lincoln, and Mercedes-Benz.

Sporty Cars
Acura Integra, Chevrolet Camaro and Corvette, Ford Mustang, Geo Storm, Honda Prelude, Mazda Miata and RX-7, Mercury Capri, Nissan 240SX, Plymouth Laser, Pontiac Firebird, Toyota Celica and MR2, and Volkswagon Cabriolet.

Sport-Utility Vehicles
These are the off-road types: Chevrolet Blazer, Ford Explorer, GMC Jimmy, Honda Passport, Isuzu Trooper and Rodeo, Jeep Cherokee and Wrangler, Mazda Navajo, Nissan Pathfinder, Oldsmobile Brevada, and Toyota Land Cruiser and 4Runner.

Vans and Trucks
These are self-classifying. You just need to decide if you want to go mini, mid-size, or full-size. What will you be using it for?

Obviously, this is not a conclusive list of everything out there, but rather a random sampling to use as a convenient way of classifying used cars. Once you do decide on the type of car you want, the next logical step would be to consider which features are for you.

OPTIONS TO CONSIDER

Buying a used car is not like buying a new car, where you can walk onto a lot and pick a car with the options you want. Usually you have to take what you can get. But do decide on what major options you want, like standard transmission or automatic, 2-door or 4-door, air conditioning, etc.

As far as the minor options, such as power windows, power steering, etc., don't get too hung up on having to buy a used car with these kinds of features. You'll only be making life very difficult for yourself when you start to shop. Just consider those minor options as window dressings. If the car happens to come with them, fine. But if it doesn't, don't let window dressings become a deciding factor in your purchase. If you do, you will be looking for a used car with just the "right" features for a long, long time.

The following is a list of options lumped together in three main categories to help you narrow your focus even further.

Passenger cars
For most passenger cars here are some things to consider: sedan, coupe, cabriolet, station wagon, hatchback, mini-van, 8-cylinder, 6-cylinder, 4-cylinder, diesel, 2-door, 4-door, automatic, standard; 4-speed or 5-speed.

Sports cars
For sports cars: coupe, convertible, hatch back, 8-cylinder, 6-cylinder, 4-cylinder, automatic, standard; 4-speed, or 5-speed.

Trucks
And for trucks: flat bed, long bed, short bed, van, utility, 1 ton, 3/4 ton, 1/2 ton, mini, mid-size, full-size, 4-wheel drive, 2-wheel drive, 8-cylinder, 6-cylinder, 4-cylinder, diesel, 2-door, 4-door, standard cab, extended cab, automatic, standard; 4-speed or 5-speed.

This should help you decide on some of the basic features that you'll be faced with. It's your choice. Once you narrow it down, for example, to a 4-door passenger sedan with a 6-cylinder engine and automatic transmission, then you are ready to head for the library.

BEST USED CAR BETS

Whether or not you already know the type of car you want, I strongly recommend something from my personal picks list. Through my own exhaustive research, I have personally selected the following to be the most reliable used cars on today's market. I took into consideration the three R's--reliability, resale value, and recall history. Please remember, how well a car has been cared for is what really decides how long it will last. Any car can end up a lemon if it was neglected for years. But leading you to cars with proven reliability will start you off on the right foot.

Small Cars
Chevrolet Cavalier 1984-'94, Chevrolet Nova 1985-'88, Dodge Colt 1980-'94, Geo Prizm 1989-'94 (previously Nova), Honda Civic 1980-'94, Mazda 323 1986-'94, Nissan Sentra 1982-'94, Plymouth Colt 1980-'94, Subaru Justy 1987-'94, Toyota Corolla 1980-'94, and Toyota Tercel 1984-'94.

Mid-Size Cars
Buick Century 1986-'94, Dodge Spirit 1989-'94 (except turbocharged), Ford Taurus (V6) 1988-'94, Honda Accord 1980-'94, Mazda Protege 1990-'94, Mazda 626 1980-'94, Mercury Sable 1988-'94, Oldsmobile Cutlass 1980-'94, Plymouth Acclaim 1989-'94, Saturn SL, SC, & SW 1991-'94, and Toyota Camry 1983-'94.

Full-Size Cars
Buick LeSabre (3.8 liter) 1985-'94, Chevrolet Caprice 1985-'94, Ford Crown Victoria 1982-'94, Mercury Grand Marquis 1983-'94, Oldsmobile Eighty-Eight 1980-'94, and Pontiac Bonneville 1980-'94.

Luxury Cars
Acura Legend 1986-'94, Lincoln Mark VII 1984-'92, Lincoln Town Car 1981-'94, Nissan Maxima 1981-'94, Toyota Cressida 1980-'92, and Volvo 240 1987-'93.

Zippy Cars
Acura Integra 1986-'94, Honda Prelude 1980-'94, Mazda Miata 1990-'94, Nissan 200/240 SX 1983-'94, and Toyota Celica 1980-'94.

Trucks/Passenger Vans/Sport Utility
Dodge Ram 50 1983-'93, Mazda Trucks 1980-'94, Nissan Trucks 1980-'94, Toyota Trucks 1980-'94, Dodge Caravan 1984-'94, Plymouth Voyager 1984-'94, Mazda MVP 1989-'94, Toyota Previa 1991-'94, Nissan Pathfinder V6 1987-'94, and Toyota 4Runner 1984-'94.

There you have it: the best of the best. Sure, there are plenty of other reliable used cars on the market, and if you choose to look for something not on my list, you won't hurt my feelings. However, for a list of additional reliable used cars, see Appendix A: **Directory of Reliable Used Cars.**

THE LIBRARY

Whether you choose some models from my list or not, I still recommend a trip to the library to find out about a car's background, like the options that were offered for a particular model, recall history, etc. The best place to start reading up on passenger cars and trucks would be in the past April issues of *Consumer Reports* magazine. Each April issue offers their annual automotive report.

Consumer Guide's annual *Used Car Book* which rates cars up to ten years old, is also a highly reputable and recommended source for used car information. *Consumer Guide* also produces two other publications that are worth a look: *Car Comparisons* and *50 Best New Cars*. Both are published once a year. Another source of information is *Kiplinger's Personal Finance Magazine,* which used to be *Changing Times.* Each December issue offers new car information for the upcoming year.

Armed with the above sources, you can research a car's list price when new, its approximate current value, its reliability rating, how it performed in rigorous test drives, any frequent mechanical problems or recalls, rated fuel economy, options that were offered, its body style (from photos), and when it was redesigned.

So, when you have a couple of hours to kill, go down to your local library with plenty of loose change for photocopies and start digging. If you have narrowed the type of car you are researching down to a few models, you can save time and look them up quickly. However, if you're starting from ground zero, it may take a little longer to leaf through and read up on the many different models. If your library is not the kind that stocks back issues of periodicals on the shelf, you'll have to request the issues you want from the reference desk.

Once you focus on several autos from the model years in your price range, make photocopies of all relevent information. You'll want to keep these for later reference. One bit of advice--it is to your advantage not to get hung up on one specific make and model. Leave yourself open to two or three different models that are similar.

For example, if you really like the look of the Ford Taurus, consider the Mercury Sable. If you like Japanese and want a Toyota Camry, consider a Honda Accord or a Mazda 626 as well. You will benefit more when you start to shop because there will be more cars to choose from. More choices translates to more competition, which means a better deal is likely for you.

THE BLUE BOOK

While you're still at the library, check out what the dealer's Blue Book price is on the auto(s) you seek. Most libraries stock a Blue Book or similar price guide, so it would be wise to check yours and make some photocopies while you're there. If your library doesn't have a current Blue Book, you can always call a bank to get a quote. The bank will consider you a potential customer for an auto loan and will be very accommodating.

Edmunds Used Car Prices, which is published quarterly and goes back ten years, will most likely be at your library, too, but you would be better off picking one up at any book store for a few bucks to have as a convenient price guide as you shop around.

To get the right quote from the Blue Book or *Edmunds,* you will need to know the following:

- year, make, and model
- engine size
- standard or automatic
- 2-door or 4-door
- any special packages that were offered like sports or luxury packages, etc.
- 2-wheel drive or 4-wheel drive (if it was an option)
- and mileage

In the case of mileage, deductions are made for cars with high mileage, while value is added for those with low miles. Both price guides will quote a wholesale and retail price. The wholesale price is what you can expect to receive from a dealer for a trade-in, while the retail price is what you can expect to pay to a dealership or a private party.

Through my own experience, I find the prices in *Kelly's Blue Book* to be inflated. There is a big difference between what *Kelly's* quotes and what *Edmunds Used Car Prices* quotes for the exact same cars. The difference can be up to a thousand dollars or more depending on the model. *Edmunds* seems to be a little more realistic in their pricing.

So when you go to buy a car and see that it's selling for five hundred below book, don't think you just found a deal. It may be five hundred above what is quoted in *Edmunds. Kelly's Blue Book* is great if you're selling a car, but not when you're buying. So my advice here is to exercise common sense. Use *Edmunds* price guide to your advantage when buying a used car and use *Kelly's Blue Book* to your advantage when selling or trading in.

Although you won't be using the inflated prices from the Blue Book to your advantage when you buy, you'll likely hear sellers quoting from it. That's the perfect time to pull out your *Edmunds* price guide and challenge them.

Keep in mind, don't let the Blue Book or *Edmunds* fool you. They are only price guides and won't fluctuate with the laws of supply and demand. If there are more buyers than product, guess what? That's right, the price goes up. Reverse the scenario--more product and less buyers--and the price goes down.

RECALL INFORMATION

The National Highway Traffic Safety Administration, under the U.S. Department of Transportation, offers a hotline number you can call for up-to-date information on recalls for any model car or truck. The number is 800-424-9393 (for the hearing impaired, the TTY number is 800-424-9153). They need to know the year, make, and model and, at your request, will send you a printout on the car via fax or mail.

Also, each auto manufacturer offers a computer research service making it easy to check out a specific car's recall history. You need the Vehicle Identification Number, which of course you don't have at this time, but when you do find a car you are considering, it is worth it to double check the recall history with the respective maker. I will remind you of this later on.

RESALE VALUE

Ever notice how some cars hold a better resale value while others seem to plummet? High resale value goes hand-in-hand with reliable cars. The market will tell you which cars are dependable, and when the market talks, you should listen. Don't shy away from used cars that seem pricey. In general, all the best rated cars will be commanding the best prices. It's like Darwin's theory of natural selection--survival of the fittest. And you should be pursuing them as well.

If your budget won't allow the year model you had hoped for, consider getting one that's a year or two older. Remember, when it's your turn to sell, you will still have something highly desirable for the next buyer. However, on models in which the resale value seems bargain priced, watch out! There's usually a good reason for it, and you needn't find out the hard way.

If you have decided on a model(s) from the list of reliable cars that I have previously researched in Appendix A, you may fast forward to the **Selecting a Mechanic** section on page 23. Should you choose not to take my advice on one of those reliable cars I have selected, please read the following two sections.

THE PHONE BOOK

Go to the yellow pages and look up Auto Repair. You need to call some repair shops to get a mechanic's opinion. Don't call a dealership service shop or even a private shop that specializes in the kind of car you're after. They may give you a biased opinion, regardless of the truth. The kind of shop you want to call is one that's been around a few years and works on a variety of domestic and foreign cars. This way you know you're getting the opinion of someone who sees a broad range of vehicles day in and day out.

When you call, ask for a mechanic and give the year, make, and model car you're thinking of buying. Ask if there are any bum years put out by the maker that you should avoid. Also ask if there was a certain engine size or feature that you should avoid in these models. You may hear responses like "the turbo-charged 4-cylinder engines in the '82 through '86 models are junk, but the 6-cylinder with fuel injection offered those same years seem to be holding out."

If you're researching for an import, be it Japanese, German, or whatever, make sure you ask about parts availability. If you live in or around a big city, chances are you'll be okay, but if you live in a small town out in the heartland, you could have problems getting parts. And since most of us don't have a week to wait for a part to come in while our car is down, this is a major consideration.

Finally, ask the mechanic for his personal opinion of these particular models. He may highly recommend them, or he may point you toward a different model altogether. Remember, he is up to his elbows in engine repair all day and sees it all, so listen to what he has to say. To get a well-rounded opinion, call at least three different repair shops.

Be careful of a mechanic who immediately tries to sell you something. Sometimes they buy, repair, and sell cars on the side. When you call to get their opinion and they just happen to have that particular model for sale, chances are they have several different cars as well and your honest mechanic may suddenly turn into Dishonest John's Used Cars. Now, the 4-cylinder turbo-charged engine becomes a spunky engine that's great on gas.

Yet, on the other hand, he could be an honest mechanic who avoids the lemons and concentrates on fixing and selling the less problematic cars. Whatever the case may be, just thank him for the tip and mention that you will keep him in mind. You're not ready to make your move yet. The key to making a good auto investment is completing your research.

WORD OF MOUTH

It may sound silly, but asking around is a good way to get an honest opinion straight from the horse's mouth. People aren't afraid to tell you their likes or dislikes about a car they own or have owned. So, ask for an honest opinion from any family, friends, or neighbors who drive the type of cars you're considering.

And now that you're familiar with the cars you seek, you should be able to spot them around town. So, in your daily travels, look for those cars that are on your list and, when the opportunity arises, whether it's at a gas station or the mall parking lot, just come out and ask the owner about his or her car.

You have your choice of approaches. You could ask "I'm thinking about buying one of those new. Have you had any problems with yours?" Or you could just try the honest approach: "I'm looking into getting one of those used. Have you had any problems with yours?" Make sure you find out the year, engine size, and how long the owner's had it so you can take all that into account. Obviously, the opinion of someone who has owned a car a few years holds more credit than the opinion of someone who's had the same car just a few months. If the person has owned it since new or for a number of years, another good question to ask is, "Would you buy another one?"

The thing about the honest approach is that the owner may have a bucket of problems and could see your interest as an opportunity to sell. Any car, regardless of how well it's rated, can end up being a lemon. He, or the previous owner(s), may not have taken care of the car and it's starting to show its neglect. So be wary of anyone suddenly trying to sell you their "great car." If it's so great, then why are they trying to unload it so quick? NEVER BE IN A HURRY TO BUY A USED CAR!

SELECTING A MECHANIC

If you don't already have a mechanic you like or trust and don't have any recommendations from your friends or family, this is what you do. Go through the yellow pages and look under Auto Repair and find several independent shops who work on the type of cars you have targeted. Call each and tell them you are looking to buy a used car and are wondering what they would charge to check it over and compression test it. They should charge no more than an hour for labor (currently around $50).

Also ask how much notice they need to set an appointment once you locate a car. You'd be better off with a mechanic who says he can take it within a day. Once you find a car you like, you don't want to be waiting more than a day to get it inspected or you could lose the sale to someone else. The way to foolproof this would be to have two or three mechanics to call on. If one is too busy, you can call the next one on your list.

SCAN THE ADS

You need to start scanning the ads for used car prices long before you're ready to buy. This is the most accurate way to see what the market is commanding for the year, make, and model you've been researching. This will also help place yourself when figuring how new a car you can afford.

Keep in mind, I am not talking about used car dealership ads. Forget about those. I'm talking about private party ads by people like you and me who are selling a car on their own. The best place to start looking is in the classifieds in your daily newspaper. Weekly "penny saving" flyers that come in the mail or can be found at the grocery store will also advertise used cars. Have a look around at your local convenience store and grocery store for special auto seller publications. Many are photo ads so you can see a picture of the car that's for sale.

Other places worth checking are public bulletin boards posted around grocery stores, hardware stores, post offices, or wherever there's heavy foot traffic. People will post "For Sale" ads, making this a great way to find a deal.

Before I have you rummaging through the auto ads, let's brush up on the typical classified abbreviations used to save space. I know most of this is just common sense, but I still want to run through it quickly so there are no questions later. Here's how some words may appear:

air conditioning - AC, air, air cond
anti-lock brakes - ABS, alb, anti lk brks
automatic transmission - AT or auto
cassette stereo - cass str
chrome - chrm
convertible - conv
coupe - cpe
custom - cust
eight-cylinder engine - 8cyl, V8
extended cab - extd cab, extra cab, x-cab, cab +
four-cylinder engine - 4cyl
four door - 4dr
four wheel drive - 4wd, FWD
fuel injection - FI
hatchback - HB, hatch
longbed - LB
manual transmission - MT, man, manual
miles per gallon - MPG
or best offer - OBO
overdrive - OD
package - pkg
paint - pnt
pickup truck - PU
power brakes - PB, pwr brks
power door locks - PL, PDL, pwr dr lks
power steering - PS, pwr st
power windows - PW, pwr wds
sedan - sdn
shortbed - SB
six-cylinder engine - 6cyl, V6, straight 6
standard transmission - ST, std, 4-speed, 5-spd
station wagon - SW, st wgn, wagon
sunroof - snrf, sun, or moonroof - mnrf
tilt steering wheel - tilt
two door - 2dr
two wheel drive - 2wd
wheels - whls
65,000 miles - 65mi, 65m, 65k

Okay, I think you get the picture, but while we're at it I would like to offer some definitions to common classified terminology to help clear the air.

Asking - Whenever you see the word "asking" preceding the price, i.e. "asking $4,500," it translates to: the seller is hoping to get close to $4,500, but is open to lower offers. "Asking" is a green light to negotiating.

Cabriolet - Just a fancy French word for convertible.

Cherry Condition or Cherry - see Mint.

Clean - It's supposed to mean that the body is dentless and rustless and there is no oil leakage from the engine or transmission. But for some, clean just means they went to the car wash before listing it for sale.

Coupe - a two-door hard-top auto with a trunk.

Custom or Customized - whenever you see this word it means not original. It could be bad or it could be good, depending on the item itself. Most of us wouldn't mind a customized stereo, but a custom sunroof can leak and hurt the value of a car.

Mint Condition or Mint - means that the car looks just like it did when it rolled off the assembly line. Unfortunately, this is rarely the case.

Factory - you may see this from time to time. A "factory sunroof" or "factory rims" means the car came that way from the factory. Factory parts are generally more desirable than custom, thereby making the auto more valuable.

Firm - means the price stated is non-negotiable. However, I have negotiated firm prices many times.

Excellent Condition - almost, but not quite mint.

Good Condition - not excellent.

Okay Condition or Looks Okay - translates to used, abused, bruised, beat-up, and thrashed. Don't even waste your time.

Needs TLC - supposed to mean needs Tender Loving Care, but what it really means is needs Time, Labor, and Cash. Avoid like the plague.

Negotiable - means that the owner is willing to go lower than the price stated.

Original - you see this word a lot in ads for older vehicles. A car that's "all original" or in "original condition" has all the original parts from the engine down to the doormats. Anything that has been removed, lost, or broken should have been replaced with an original part.

Original Owner or One Owner - means that the car has had the same owner since new. These are the ones to look for. One owner means less chance for abuse.

Runs Excellent - self-explanatory.

Runs Good - doesn't run excellent.

Runs - basically means the engine runs, but is on its last leg. If you see an ad that says "runs," run away from it.

Sedan - a 2- or 4-door hard-top auto with a trunk.

Keep in mind, the prices you see advertised are padded. It doesn't mean the seller will actually get that. So consider this: If you have $2,000 to buy a new car and you see many '86s of the model you want selling in the $2,200 to $2,500 range, then you are right in the ball park. You can always count on sellers increasing the price of their autos hundreds above what they would actually take. We'll discuss this in detail in the negotiation chapter. In the meantime, don't let over-priced cars in a certain year lead you to believe that you can't afford one.

For those of us who live in a small town where there isn't much of a used car market, all this can be difficult to do. But if there's a larger city an hour or two away, it would be a good idea to check out the market there. You can do this without driving there if the city's paper and auto publications are available in your town. When it comes time to go look at cars, it could be well worth the one-or two-hour trip to find a decent car at a reasonable price. If you don't already have one, this would be a good time to get a city street map to make it easier to find your way around.

FINANCING

The best way to buy a car is with a lump-sum of cash. However, if you don't have the money saved up in a nest or have a rich uncle to schmooze, you'll be at the bank's mercy and must borrow--like the rest of us. If such is the case, financing becomes a big part of your research. Find out up front how much car you can afford and get pre-approved with a finance company that offers a competitive Annual Percentage Rate (APR). This way you will know how much the loan will cost you, the amount of your monthly payment, and the length of term BEFORE you go used car shopping. Finding an auto loan that fits you is like finding a car that fits you; you have to shop around. Some loan companies offer better deals than others.

The best way to finance your car is through a home equity loan. If you're a homeowner, check with your bank to see if you have enough equity to finance the amount you need for a car. The advantage in doing this allows you to deduct the interest payments at the end of the year, whereas in a conventional auto loan you can not.

If you belong to an employee credit union, this would also be an excellent source to check for low rates. If you don't own a home or belong to a credit union, find the best rate you can through the commercial banks and get yourself set up with one. If later you decide to go the dealership route, you can check what rates the dealership has to offer to see if they can beat the company you're with. Some do offer competitive rates.

Most banks and finance companies like to see 20% down (depending on the year of the car) on a used car loan. If you can come up with more, it is to your advantage. I recommend putting down as much as you can and financing as little as possible. It will mean lower monthly payments or a shorter term and, most importantly, less interest to pay in the long run.

If you do decide to finance through a dealership, watch out for loans boasting no money down and/or no payments for 90 days, etc. They sound tempting, but you'll only be burying yourself deeper into debt. Dealers will get the monthly payment really low for you, but you may end up paying interest on your interest or adding an extra year of payments to your loan. This translates to more money in the dealer's and finance company's pockets and less in yours. More information on dealership financing is covered in the **Dealing With Dealers** chapter.

AUTO INSURANCE

Insurance is expensive these days, thanks to frauds and ambulance-chasing lawyers convincing accident victims to sue for outrageous sums for their "pain and suffering." And with a $30,000 car not an uncommon thing these days, the rising cost of autos has also contributed to the steep premiums we all pay.

If you are a first-time car buyer or making a drastic change from your previous auto, like going from a pickup truck to a sports car, you better get an estimate on insurance BEFORE you buy. Most of us do not like surprises and you may be surprised, unpleasantly, after you purchase that 'Vette and find yourself short when you go to insure it.

The best place to start checking for good rates would be through your homeowner's insurance policy--if you're a homeowner, that is. If not, find out which company your parents are with. Most agencies will offer family discounts on auto insurance policies.

Otherwise, the only other advice I can give here is to shop around. Surf the yellow pages and dial until your finger goes numb. Not all insurance agencies are created equal, as you will find when you receive a wide range of quotes. Go with the lowest from a reputable company.

THE EIGHT GOLDEN RULES OF RESEARCH

1) Focus on at least two models that suit your needs
2) Read up on them at the library, finding out as much as possible
3) Get the book price quotes from the Blue Book and *Edmunds* or a similar price guide
4) Touch base with a couple of mechanics for future inspections
5) Study the classified ads and learn the market on the cars you seek
6) Get your finances in order
7) Know what insurance will cost
8) Never be in a hurry to buy a used car

CHAPTER 2:

THE SEARCH

ARE YOU READY?

Have you narrowed your focus down to two or three particular models? Do you know which features you want? Do you know what the wholesale and retail prices are in a Blue Book and *Edmunds*? Did you read every auto classified publication you could get your hands on to learn what the going market is on the year models you desire? Did you get yourself lined up with at least one reliable mechanic? Is your financing all set to go at a moment's notice? Did you call and get some quotes from several insurance agents? Have you read my book all the way through, made notes accordingly, and understood clearly what is being presented? If you have, your research is complete. You are now ready to start the search.

Because you've already been scanning the ads, you know where to look for possible leads. By this time you should already know on which days weekly publications come out. Make a point to get the publication as soon as it's published. If a particular auto seller comes out every Friday, you don't want to be in town picking up a copy on Thursday. The ads are already a week old, and you will find that many cars have already sold. Quite often people sell cars well below market value because they are in dire need for some quick cash or they don't realize their car's full worth.

Remember, the dealers read the same ads and are constantly hunting for a kill. You are not hunting for a kill, but you are hunting for a reasonable deal--and sometimes even those go quickly.

INTERPRETING AN AD

Let's say you are looking for a Honda Accord and you come across a classified ad which reads:

> **'89 Honda Accord LX** - 4 dr,
> 5spd, low mi, looks and runs
> like new $6,800 call 555-5555

Now, because you have done your research, you know the LX is the luxury edition with all the goodies. What you don't know is how many miles the car has or it's real condition. Even though the ad says "low miles," your idea of low miles for an '89 might not be the same as that of the seller's. "Looks and runs like new" also sounds good, but again, your idea of something that looks and runs like new may not coincide with the seller's.

I once looked at a car which supposedly "looked like new" that had been hit in the rear fender. When I questioned the seller about his misleading ad, this was his reply: "Except for the dent, everything looks like new. Just look at that interior, not even a crack in the dash!"

The price of $6,800 is reasonable because you know what the fair market value of an '89 Accord is, thanks to your research. This ad is worth a phone call and that's something that takes only two seconds to decide.

QUESTIONS TO ASK

When you call, greet the owner politely and always reread the ad back to him. "I'm calling about the Accord. That's an '89 LX?..." Get into the habit of doing this just to double check that there hasn't been a misprint on the paper's behalf. You wouldn't want to drive an hour to look at what you thought was going to be an '89 Accord and have it turn out to be a '79.

"**How many miles are on it?**" would be the next question to ask. You can figure about 12,000 to 15,000 miles a year is average. The '89, being six years old, should have less than 72,000 miles if the ad said low miles. Always ask this question whether the ad says anything about mileage or not. Mileage is a key indicator of how much wear is on the engine. If the car's been properly maintained, we can assume the less miles on it, the more life it has left. But if an engine has been rebuilt or replaced, then the mileage doesn't apply.

Keep in mind, any car with a new or rebuilt engine that isn't more than eight years old has either had a hard life or is a poor design to begin with, and you didn't complete your research. In either case, stay away. Other costly repairs are just around the corner.

"**How long have you owned it?**" A very important question. If the person has owned it since new, then you are speaking to the original owner. Originally owned cars are highly desired over multiple-owner cars. Why? A multiple owner-car is more likely to have been neglected by an uncaring owner at some point in its life. How would you know for sure if the oil was changed on schedule or if the engine was properly tuned?

With multiple owners, you'll never know for sure about the car's past, but with an original owner, you'll be able to find out about the whole life of the car. That's not to say that all originally owned cars have been well cared for, but if they weren't, you'll know as soon as you see the car. Years of neglect will be staring you in the face.

In all the single-owner cars I have come across I can't recall one that was in bad shape. I guess original owners are just a special breed. They buy a brand new car with the intention of keeping it for a long time, so they take good care of it. A one-owner car is what you want. It's what the dealers want. It's what everybody wants.

If the owner has not owned it since new, ask if he bought it from the original owner. He may be the second or even third owner and know the previous owner(s) and what they were like. These are the kinds of things you like to hear when calling about used cars.

If it turns out that the owner has only had the car for a short period and doesn't know how many previous owners there were, then we are looking at a car blind. You can still buy a decent car blindly, you just have to be extra careful about it. A car that has changed a lot of hands may have something wrong with it that is expensive to fix. Which leads us to our next question.

"**Why are you selling it?**" Always assume that people are selling cars because there's something wrong with them. I know this seems like a paranoid way of thinking, but I want you to think this way to protect yourself. Many people will own a car until the engine starts leaking or the clutch starts slipping or the tires wear out or a combination of problems start adding up.

Instead of fixing the problem(s), they decide to buy a new car and let the next owner deal with it. Why put money into their car if they are about to sell it anyway? But in order to get the best price they will try to hide the car's faults and THEY WILL LIE TO YOU ABOUT THEIR CAR'S CONDITION. So don't believe what they say. Believe what your common sense and your mechanic say.

People can always lie about why they're selling their car, but more times than not you'll be able to detect if they're being honest with you. This is a question you'll ask twice: once over the phone and once when you look at the car. Notice if the second response differs from the first. If possible, try and ask a different person the second time to see if his or her answers coincide. For example, ask the wife over the phone the first time, and the husband in person the second time, etc.

People have all kinds of reasons to sell a car. The ones we like to hear are, "I'm selling it because I just bought a new car." Rather than trade in their used model to a dealer, many owners choose to sell their cars privately because they can get more money on their own. Remember, dealers are going to mark up a trade-in to make a profit, so they can only offer so much, which is well below market value. The new-car excuse is the one you'll most likely hear from an original owner.

Another good reason which can also give you some bargaining muscle is if someone is moving. These people may be desperate, especially if their phones aren't ringing. So keep your eyes peeled for "moving, must sell" ads. Sometimes people come into a tight money situation and, for one reason or another, they need to liquidate their car for cash. They are having a baby or they got laid off. Whatever the reason, as long as it's justified, you can rest easy when it's a person problem and not a car problem.

If the seller says he's bought something else, which is also used, it may be just his personal taste, but it could also be because the car has been nothing but a money pit and he needs to unload it. Other excuses to be nervous about are ones like "I don't need it anymore" or "I want to upgrade." Any excuse with this type of tone is a good indication of a car that people are unhappy with, so be wary.

"Is everything working" or "Is there anything broken that needs to be fixed?" These are good questions to ask. Today, cars are loaded up with so much power gadgetry you want to know if everything is working properly ahead of time (cruise control, air-conditioning, power windows, etc.).

Even though you'll double check all this stuff when you inspect the car, ask up front anyway. If something is broken you can call the dealership ahead of time and get a phone estimate for the MAXIMUM amount it could cost to fix. Then, if you decide to make an offer on the car, you use this repair cost as bargaining leverage.

"Has the car ever been in an accident?" People can easily lie about this one, but there are ways to look for hidden body damage that we will discuss later. If an owner admits to a fender bender over the phone, ask for the details. If the car has just been bumped slightly with only minor damage, then it's still worth a look.

However, if the car has had major damage, stay away. Once a car's frame has been bent it is very difficult to get it back to the way it was. Cars that have been hit commonly have alignment problems that are unrepairable. The end result may be tires wearing out much too fast, rough cornering, and steering wheel shimmy.

"Are you negotiable in your price?" Always ask this over the phone. Most of the time the response will be something like "I'll negotiate a little" or "Yes, I need to sell it." Judging by the way they answer can tip you off as to how low an offer you dare make.

If you've read my definitions, then you know that ads which read "firm" mean the seller doesn't want to budge on the price, but don't let this stop you from making an offer a couple of hundred dollars less. Firm to some people means they'll only sell their car two hundred less rather than five hundred. It never hurts to ask. The worst thing that could happen is that they say no. The best thing that could happen is that you save yourself a couple of Ben Franklins. You'd be surprised how many times it has worked for me.

"Has anyone else looked at it yet?" and "How long have you had it for sale?" Like all the other questions, people can lie about these too. But if the owner seems honest this far in your conversation, ask if anyone else has seen the car yet. What we want to hear is "No, you'll be the first." This means that the car on the market is a virgin and you are in line for a first look. Why is this good?

A car that has been on the market for a week or longer and had three or more lookers indicates that either there's something wrong with it or the car is over-priced. If a car has had one or two people look at it and pass, it's still worth a look. They could have just been a couple of looky-loos who really weren't ready to buy or are having financing problems, etc. But when you get up to three or more previous lookers and the car still hasn't sold, it's almost a guarantee that there is something wrong with it.

If you have some extra time, go have a look. And be careful. When you go to inspect it, keep asking yourself this question: "Why hasn't this car sold yet?"

OTHER QUESTIONS TO ASK

"How much are you asking?" Even if the ad states their price in bold letters, ask this question anyway. Their response can give you clues to how negotiable they are. "I'm asking $5,500, but open to offers," "The price in the ad is $4,300, but I'd probably take $4,000". This is a form of preconditioning in which I go into detail in the **Negotiation** chapter.

If there isn't a price stated in the ad then you definitely want the answer to this before making an appointment. Don't let someone play games with you on this either. Sometimes people will try to get you to come out and look first, then talk price. If anyone tries this with you, just tell them you're not coming over until you know what their asking price is.

"Do you have any service records or receipts for work done to the car?" If they do, ask them to have them available for you to look at when you come over. Also ask if any major repairs have been performed like brakes, clutch, etc.

"Who did the maintenance?" If the seller did his own oil changes, ask if he kept a ledger or service record. If he did, ask to have it available for you to see as well. If he didn't, don't believe him when he tells you he changed the oil every 3,000 miles. I say this with confidence because the type of people who change their oil every 3,000 miles are not the type of people who don't make record of it.

"Does the car have a salvage title?" If the car seems bargain priced, nine times out of ten this is the reason. Nothing's worse than putting in the time and effort to find a car, only to learn that it has a salvage title right before you are about to transfer ownership. For more information on what a salvage title is, turn to page 82. But you can trust me right here and now. You don't want to buy a car with a salvage title. You want a car with a clean title.

"Are you the owner?" If the person selling the car is not the owner, suspect that the seller is a dealer, at least a part-time one, probably selling cars one at a time from his house. If this is the case, be extra careful when checking over the car and don't believe a word he says. He may have bought it at an auction or from someone out of the paper the week before and knows nothing about the car's history, even though he may tell you he is selling it for his "cousin," who took excellent care of it.

Listen to how the seller talks. Does he seem pretty smooth with what he is saying like he's done this many times before, or does he sound awkward and unsure of himself? If he seems well rehearsed, figure him to be a dealer. Call your local motor vehicle department to see if there are any additional forms you or the seller must fill out when a third party is involved in the transfer of title.

GET AN APPOINTMENT

If you decide the car is worth a look, set up an appointment to see the car as soon as possible. Within an hour is preferable. I know this is impossible for most, because of work and all, but try to arrange it so when you are calling on used car ads you have time to go and look as soon as you hang up the phone.

Consider the following scenarios: You come home from work on Friday with the latest auto seller publication. You scan through the ads and find a car you've been looking for. You don't wait until tomorrow to call because dinner is at 7 p.m. and after that it'll be too late. You're going to call right now. You talk to the person for about 15 minutes, drilling him with questions, and everything sounds good so far. You tell him you want to come look at it now, and he agrees to meet with you in an hour.

You get there 15 minutes early with $50 to $100 (or your checkbook) in your pocket. You spend about 45 minutes to inspect and test drive the car. Everything seems okay. You negotiate a fair price with the understanding that you want to have your mechanic check it out first thing tomorrow morning (much more on this later). You leave a $50 deposit which will be refunded if the car doesn't pass your mechanic's inspection. Should your mechanic find only minor problems, you will be allowed to either pass or renegotiate to a lower price with the seller. You come home late for dinner, excited and hungry.

The next morning you meet at your mechanic's shop, where he carefully inspects it. Except for some brakes that will soon need replacing, everything checks out. You're ready to buy the car as is, but because of the brakes, you try to bargain him down further in price. The owner, who saw the report from the mechanic, agrees and you save yourself more money and end up with a car that lets you sleep peacefully at night.

For those of you who must drive to a nearby city, the situation is slightly different. You are setting up two or more appointments for first thing Saturday morning. You want to make it worthwhile to make that drive, and hopefully you'll only need to give up a couple of Saturdays until you score.

This is how cars are bought. You have to absorb some inconveniences in your personal life, like missing dinner or giving up your weekend, but with some time and effort, you will be rewarded. Isn't this how most things work in life?

EXCUSES, EXCUSES

That's what you'll need to escape from some of the clunkers you will find yourself looking at. No matter how well you screen them over the phone, you will still get stuck looking at a "beater." But a good excuse gets you out of there quickly and politely. Whether you just started looking or have been looking for months, don't go car shopping without a good excuse for a quick escape.

- "I just started looking, and I want to see what else
  is around before I make any decisions."
- "I have two others to look at, and I want to see
  those before I make any decisions."

What you don't want to do is upset someone by telling him what you really think of his car. Call it diplomacy, call it lying, but in a gun-happy society where people shoot you for looking at them wrong, I call it surviving.

For telephone excuses, don't tell someone you're coming over to look at his car when you have no intentions of doing so. I find many people do this just to get off the phone. There's nothing more rude than telling someone you'll be there at a certain time and then not showing. You're wasting their time, and they may be scheduling appointments with serious buyers around yours. Have the decency to tell them you're not interested when you're really not. If you're afraid of hurting someone's feelings, you can always say:

- "You know, I really wanted an automatic," or "You know, I really wanted a five-speed." In other words, whatever their car has, you wanted the opposite.
- "It doesn't sound like what I want. I'm going to have to pass."

If you talk to someone on the phone who seems real anxious to sell you his car and you can tell already that it's not something you want, use the excuse I use.

- "I have a couple other ads that I want to call before I start setting up any appointments. I'll call you back when I'm ready to come by."

There's something about eager beaver sellers. The more anxious they are to get me over there, the more I don't want to go. It usually means there's something wrong with their car, and they will try some fast talking to keep from losing you. Lose them instead.

CARS WITH OUT-OF-STATE PLATES

I see it all the time. A car with an out-of-state plate selling for a bargain price. But there's usually a reason why. If you're considering a car from out of state, you'd better find out exactly what the registration and/or emission regulations are in your home state BEFORE you purchase.

Here in California, where emissions are very strict, we have what is known as a smog impact fee for out-of-state vehicles. The fee is $300 and there's no way around it if you want to register the car in California. On top of that is the smog inspection. If the out-of-state car had any emission components removed that are required here in California, but not required in the state from which the car originated, you will have to put them back on, no matter what the cost. This could get into lots of dough. Vehicles from out of state may also need special attention for rust or flood damage.

Other states may have similar fees for registering out-of-state vehicles, so if you're on a really tight budget it would be wise to find this out in advance. Call your motor vehicle department or state certified inspection center (if your state has them) and ask. All they need to know is the year of the model you wish to register, and they can tell you what the requirements were for that year. Don't forget to add any extra registration charges to your bargaining list.

This is just one of those things you want to be aware of when used car shopping. It's a good idea for California residents to find a mechanic who also does smog inspections so he can make sure everything is up to snuff. You don't want any surprises later.

CITY MILES VS. FREEWAY MILES

Here in California, where you must drive the freeways to get anywhere, it's common to find cars approaching the 200,000 mile mark that are still running fine. At the same time, it's possible to find cars that were driven primarily in city traffic, such as a delivery service, etc., which require engine work before reaching 90,000 miles. Considering both vehicles receive the same service intervals, why does one engine easily outlast the other?

It's simple. Most engine wear occurs during cold engine start-up and through frequent stop-and-go driving. Cars that are driven on the freeway at constant speeds experience minimal engine wear. Look at it this way: A person who does a daily freeway round trip of 50 miles only cold starts his engine twice and drives a few stop-and-go miles to and from the freeway. Whereas, a delivery driver who services a 50-mile route will start his engine dozens of times, and be subject to stop-and-go traffic during the entire route.

If a car you're looking at has high miles and you can verify that they are mostly freeway miles, don't let it keep you from buying. But watch out for cars that were subject to city driving, no matter how many miles they may have.

DON'T BE HASTY

If you ever get frustrated in your search and become tempted to take the used car dealership route, here are some things you should consider. Used car dealers get many of their cars from auto auctions. Have you ever wondered where the auctions get these cars?

Some come from businesses that were used for delivery fleets. Some come from car rental agencies who unload them after a certain number of miles to avoid costly repairs. Some are repossessions that come from banks who are trying to cut their losses on defaulted loans by irresponsible owners. If someone wasn't responsible enough to make his payments, do you think he was responsible enough to service his car regularly? In each case you're looking at cars that either have a) high miles; b) been driven hard; c) been neglected; or d) all of the above.

In addition, dealers will go to these auctions and listen to cars run but won't drive them. Because you can't find out about a transmission problem, or a clutch that's about to go out, or an irreparable alignment that wears down a 40,000 mile tire in 8,000 miles by listening to the engine, it's common for dealers to get stuck with a dog. Now, what do you suppose they are going to do with those dogs? You don't think a dealer is going to absorb a loss, do you? He's going to pass it on to you.

Don't forget that dealers also buy autos right out of the classifieds from private parties and then turn around and sell them for much more. These are cars that are available to you just as easy as they are to them. The difference is you could save hundreds up front on the purchase price and possibly thousands later in costly repairs when you buy from a private party.

Even though most new car dealerships who take trade-ins may have some decent used cars on their lot, you won't find any at a reasonable price. Dealers work off commissions, and they know the market. They are into making money, and you won't get too far with them at the negotiation table. So only take the dealership route as a last resort.

DANGLING CARROTS

One last thing: In your travels through the classifieds you may see dealers advertising cars at unbelievably low prices or financing offers that sound too good to be true. That's usually because they are. Dealers play con games to get you onto their lot.

The old "bait and switch" is a favorite. In the paper you see Honest John's Used Cars is advertising a certain car for a really low price. Frustrated with the classifieds, you go down to check it out. When you inquire about the ad car you'll hear something like, "We just sold it an hour ago, but we have these similar models over here that just came in." You can bet your sweet bippi they won't be for the same price, though.

With the financing carrot, you see an advertisement from Crazy Joe's Deals on Wheels that claims zero down with 100% percent financing at only 4.9% interest. Now you say to yourself, "That's much better than buying a car through my bank," so you race down to Crazy Joe's to inquire about the ad and a friendly salesman acknowledges and starts showing you around. You find a car you like and test drive it while the salesman assures you what a great deal you'll be getting. You want the car, and you go into the sales office (shark pit) to negotiate and close the deal.

If you're not paying attention it may go right over your head, but if you're on your toes you notice the 4.9% interest has somehow grown to 12%. So you stop him and ask about the ad, and you get something like, "Oh, that's just for first-time buyers," or "It's just for senior citizens," or "It's for people with excellent credit," or "It's for people with no credit." Are you starting to catch on?

Whatever your situation is, the 4.9% loan will be for those with the opposite features. In reality, the 4.9% deal just doesn't exist. It's just a hook. And now you are hooked because you find this out after having spent hours inspecting, test driving, and negotiating a price with the dealer. By this time you want the car bad and you're not about to let a couple of silly interest points stand in you way. This is just another one of the many ways the dealer can get you--hook, line, and sinker. So the moral of the dealer story is, if it sounds too good to be true, it is.

THE SEVEN GOLDEN RULES OF THE SEARCH

1) Read the ads religiously
2) Know the right questions to ask
3) Learn how to interpret their responses
4) Set up an appointment as soon as possible
5) Memorize polite excuses
6) Avoid dealers like the plague
7) Never be in a hurry to buy a used car

CHAPTER 3:

CHECKING OUT THE BEAST

The first time you read this chapter, just read through and go with the flow. There's no way I expect you to remember all this stuff, which is why I have included an inspection checklist in Appendix B (page 168). Before you go car hunting, make some photocopies for your reference. This will help you to remember all those steps and keep you from overlooking anything.

When you have made an appointment to look at your first car, go with the thought in mind that it won't be your last. The chances that you buy the first car you look at are unlikely, unless you didn't listen to what I wrote and get swept off your feet by your favorite color.

SOME FIRSTHAND TIPS

When looking at used cars, wear clothes you don't mind getting dirty. You'll be poking around the engine and getting down on your knees as well. And bring a rag, too. You'll most likely get some grease on your fingers.

Always show up 15-30 minutes before the time you had set. If they say come over at 3 o'clock, you show up between 2:30 and

2:45. Why do this? Because you want to see if they are adding fresh oil or wiping up oil drops from the garage floor or adding air to that slow-leaking tire or running the car and driving it around because it starts better when warmed up. You get the picture? By showing up early, sometimes you can catch them in the act of hiding something they don't want you to know about.

Also, make it a point to look at a car during the day. You want to see what a car's paint and body look like in the daylight, not under artificial light or in poor lighting. Things just don't look the same under artificial lighting. Many people I know, myself included, have bought autos that were inspected at night only to find the morning sun revealing some body waves that we could have sworn weren't there the night before.

If you're looking at cars during the winter months when it gets dark early, you could inspect them on weekends or maybe slip away from your job during lunch hour to have a look. If you do look at night and you like the car, look at it once more in the daylight before closing the deal. You may be glad you did.

Always make it a point to look at a car with a cold engine. First thing in the morning would be the optimum time, but I know this isn't always possible. The reason for this is that you want to see how the car starts on a cold engine. Is the choke in adjustment, or does the engine cough and stall?

Most importantly, listen for worn lifters. While the engine is cold, worn lifters will be talking to you loud and clear with a terrible knocking sound coming from the top of the engine. But once oil circulates and has a chance to coat the lifters, the sound becomes deadened and magically disappears. This can even slip by your mechanic, since you warm up the engine driving to his shop. Replacing eight lifters on a 4-cylinder motor can run $300, so request a cold engine before you go over to look.

And one last note: Bring a flashlight. Even during the day, you need a flashlight to check the engine for oil seepage, and you will want to look around underneath the car as well. You should already carry a flashlight in your car for emergencies, so if you don't, now is a good time to get one. If you do keep one in your car, make sure it's working properly BEFORE you go used car shopping.

A WORD ABOUT COLOR

Color is the last thing to consider when buying a used car, but it is a consideration. You don't have to be Einstein to understand that, especially in the summer, darker colors make a car hotter than lighter colors. What most people don't realize, however, is that darker colors, especially black, show dirt more, whereas lighter colors, especially white, make dirt invisible.

How can this be? It's simple. Light colors reflect light and dark colors absorb light. When dirt and dust settle on a white car and the sun is beating down reflecting a light-colored surface, the dirt becomes practically invisible to the eye. But when dirt and dust settle on a black surface, the color of the dirt will be easily reflected from the sun absorbing color. That's why it's so hard to keep a black car clean.

It is preferable to buy a used car with its original paint job, which should be the case for any car up to ten years old. I'd rather buy a ten-year-old car that needs a paint job than a ten-year-old car that has just been painted.

Why? Because with an original paint job I know exactly where the body's at with rust, accidents, etc., whereas with the new paint job, I can only guess. If there were some small rust holes in the body and the car had been worked on by professionals, you and I won't know where the holes were for at least another year until the rust starts to bubble back through. You see, once rust has eaten a hole in your car it can never be stopped, it can only be slowed down. New paint scares me. It usually means a car that's been in an accident or has serious rust, neither of which I want.

One more thing, avoid color-changed cars. If the car has been repainted, you want the color to be the same as that of the original. If the paint is a custom color, the car loses value. Why? Because most people are turned off by custom colors. So even though you think that pink VW looks cool, keep in mind when it's your turn to sell, you'll find out just how unique you are when countless people pass on it, and you're forced to lower the price well below market value.

HOW TO CHECK FOR BODY DAMAGE FROM AN ACCIDENT

Three of the simplest ways for revealing evidence of a car that has been either the hitter or hittee is by checking for overspray and mismatched paint, eyeballing a car's body and seams, and inspecting the car's frame.

Although it's no guarantee, most repainted cars are repainted because the owner received a check on his insurance claim from an accident. Think about it. Cars are rarely painted because someone has an extra $1,500 laying around and they suddenly want a new gloss.

Look closely for overspray around all the window seals and lights and other trim. If the car was repainted, it usually doesn't take long to find where the tape didn't cover a sliver of the window seal, indicating new paint. Another good place to check for overspray is in the engine compartment. If the car had a color change, you may find its original color here. With your flashlight handy, look at the wheel wells alongside the engine and the fire wall (behind the engine). Look for overspray on wires and hoses. The trunk is another place to look if you suspect a color change. Pull up the floor mat in the trunk and you will see the car's original color. Weather stripping around the doors and trunk will usually catch a little overspray, revealing new paint.

Mismatched paint is a definite indication of a car that's been in an accident. This is where a car has had some body parts replaced, such as a fender and hood, and then just the new parts get sprayed with the original color. Only problem is, a car that is a few years old is going to have sun-faded, ozone-oxidized paint that won't be as deep in color or as shiny as the new body parts. Mismatched paint is difficult to notice at night, which is why you should look at a car in broad daylight. To make sure that all fenders, doors, and hoods match, you need to look at the car from all angles in the sun and in the shade without your sunglasses.

While you're doing this you can check for body waves, which will also indicate an accident. To check for waves in the body, park your eyes about three feet in front of the headlight and look down the length of the car. The front fender, doors, and rear fender should all line up straight as an arrow. Look at both sides. If you notice any waves in the sheet metal, the car has been hit. However, don't confuse body waves with door pings. A door ping will look like a dimple in the sheet metal, whereas body waves are more broad. Check the roof for body waves too. If you find any, the car has either been rolled or someone walked on the roof and dented it.

Have you ever seen that commercial for the Lexus where they roll the ball bearing down the seam that separates the fender from the hood? They are trying to impress you with the precision of a well-built car by illustrating its perfectly matching joints. This is what you will be looking at when you're checking for hidden body damage. I'm not saying to carry a marble with you to roll down the seams; don't embarrass yourself. It's easy enough just to eyeball them.

The places to look are where the hood, trunk, and doors open. With them all closed, check these seams carefully. The gap should run evenly all the way around. If you come across a seam that is wide at one end and narrow at the other, then you are looking at a car that has been hit. Question the owner about this and if he denies it was in an accident or claims he bought it that way, he is either lying or it was hit when it was with the previous owner.

If the owner admits to an accident, get the details. How much damage was there and what was replaced? Who did the body repairs? If you are looking at uneven seams, open and close the trunk or door that is in question to see how freely it works. A sticking door or a trunk that is hard to close is further evidence of a car that's been hit. If this is combined with mismatched paint, then give this car an automatic failure. However, if the seams are only a little off, nothing's sticking, and the paint matches, continue to the next step, which is checking the frame.

To check the frame, you need to get down on your hands and knees with your trusty flashlight and shine it on the underbelly of the car. The frame will be the thickest gauge metal going up and down the full length of the car, usually on both sides (depending on the car). You want to pay particular attention to this, shining your light on it all the way up and down. Check it from under both sides of the car. You're looking for anything that doesn't look right, like metal that is bent or weld marks which basically looks like melted metal. If you see something like I've just described, then, congratulations, you have verified that the car has been in an accident. AUTOMATIC FAILURE! My advice here is to quietly leave. It's not worth the gamble, buying something and hoping it is back to normal. Once a car's frame has been messed with, it may never be the same.

If everything looks okay then continue with your inspection. Please remember, even if you do miss evidence of an accident, your mechanic will catch it and can decipher its seriousness.

Another suspect for an accident, and this goes for rust as well, is one door lock that requires a different key. Most cars are made with one key that fits all locks. Check the trunk and all door locks with the ignition key. If any lock doesn't work, suspect that that door or trunk lid has been replaced. Please note that some cars come with a separate key for the trunk. Find out up front if this is the case for those cars you seek.

Unhidden body damage is easy to find because its unsightliness stares you right in the face. And, because you knew what questions to ask over the phone, you have hopefully weeded out the undesirables. But sometimes people exaggerate, fib, or lie right through their teeth, and that small dent in the fender turns out to be bashed so bad that the trunk lid has to be tied down. Of course, at this point you want to strangle the person for bringing you here and wasting your time. If this should happen, grin and bear it, and politely tell them that that wasn't what you had in mind, and move on.

HOW TO CHECK FOR BODY DAMAGE FROM RUST

Unless you live near the ocean, rust isn't much of a problem here in the arid southwest. However, in the north, where they salt the roads in the winter, or in the coastal southeast, where the combination of humidity and salt air practically melts your car away, rust can be a big obstacle in used car hunting.

Rust usually starts in one of two ways. It either starts from the exterior, such as a chip in your paint exposing bare metal or, worse yet, comes from the inside and starts bubbling up through the paint. Rust that comes from the inside out is a sign of a poorly made car, but any car that is visually rusty should be avoided.

Even if you figure in the cost of body work and a paint job, once a rust hole has started it can never be stopped, only slowed down. Rust never sleeps, and usually within a year it will start bubbling back through, depreciating your car's resale value radically. If you live in a "rust belt" region, be wary of older cars that have been recently repainted. You can hide a lot of sin with body filler and paint. It is up to you to detect it.

In checking for rust, it makes sense to look in the most common problem areas. This would be around the wheel wells and the fenders immediately behind the tires where stones get kicked up, chip the paint, and expose bare metal for rust to attack. The front of the car can also catch flying stones from other cars, making this a problem area as well.

With your trusty flashlight in hand, look underneath the car behind the front and rear tires on both sides. Of course, before you do this MAKE SURE THE CAR IS PARKED ON A LEVEL SURFACE IN PARK/GEAR AND THE EMERGENCY BRAKE ENGAGED! If it's on a slope, put blocks under the wheels for added safety. Shine your light on the inside of the fenders as well as the wheel wells. You are looking for excess body filler, which from this side looks like hardened putty all globbed up.

In areas where you don't have a clear view, use your fingers as your eyes and feel around. Do you feel globs of hardened putty under there? Other rust-prone places to check would be the exterior flooring under the driver's and passenger's seats, under the carpeting/matting on the floor inside, under the carpeting/matting in the trunk, and around the engine compartment. USE YOUR FLASHLIGHT, YOUR EYES AND YOUR FINGERS!

Another way of checking areas is by using your ears. Above the area in question, tap lightly on the car's body with your knuckles. You should hear a tinny metal sound. Continue tapping and move slowly down to the area in question. Does the sound change from tinny to solid and dense? If it does, then that's further evidence of body filler and it's decision-making time for you. Would you want this car providing everything else checks out? The car may look great now, but if it looks like hell in a year, you'll be the loser in this deal.

If he hasn't already told you, ask the seller who did the body work. If he plays dumb--his car receives an automatic failure. However, if he has receipts from a well-known body shop, get the name of the shop and the person who did the body work. You need to find out how the rust was addressed. Was it ground down or completely cut away?

The grinding/sanding method is the least expensive and, consequently, most common way rust is repaired. If the rust is caught before it creates a hole in the metal, then, yes, it can be stopped. The rust is sanded away until it is bare, shiny metal, then primed and painted.

Unfortunately, most people don't notice rust on their car until it is too late. Large rust spots turn into rust holes once they face the sand blaster. After that, you are fighting a losing battle because body filler with paint on top is only a temporary solution to a permanent problem.

Yet because people want to sell their cars for the most money and the cost is relatively cheap, they get the economy paint job, which is just enough to make it look good. Or worse yet, some people will attempt the body work themselves. Trust me on this: You don't want to buy a car that looks good temporarily.

However, contrary to what you just read, there are ways to beat rust. But they are very costly and usually only used as a last-ditch effort to save a car from the auto graveyard. Such is the case on many classic car restorations.

The best way to cure a car of rust is simply by replacing that rusty fender, door, etc. with a new or rust-free salvaged part from the junkyard. Of course, if the rust has spread to the main part of the body, you're left with the second and less desirable cure: cutting out the rusty metal and welding in new pieces. The metal is then ground down and smoothed out with body filler.

When done right, the body will last just as long as it would new, and a professional can make it invisible. So if you were able to contact the body shop that worked on the car and know for a fact that the car in question was corrected in this manner, then continue on with your inspection.

TIRES AND SUSPENSION

Take a close look at all four tires. You will find information about the tire's size and type written right on its sidewalls. They should all be the same. There shouldn't be three 195s and one 225, and there should never be a mixture of radials and bias ply tires. You may see a car with a matched pair of tires on the front and a slightly larger matched pair on the rear. This is okay for now, but later you'll want to install the correct tire size for maximum safety and performance (check the owner's manual or the dealer for this information). If this is the case, figure in the cost for two new tires.

To check the tread, stick a key between the grooves in the most worn area of the tire. Put your thumb nail flush up to the tread and against the key, then remove. Anything 1/8 inch or less will require new tires within 5,000 miles. That translates to less than four months for the average driver. The cost of four new tires can run you anywhere from $200 to $500 depending on the size and quality. That's a big bill. Make a note on your checklist to find out the cost of new tires for this model. You want to keep this in mind when bargaining time comes around.

To test the shocks, go around to each corner of the car and push up and down a few times and then let go to see how much it bounces on its own. If it goes up and down more than twice, find out what the cost of a new set of shocks for this car will be and add that to your bargaining list.

To detect a suspension problem, park the car on a level surface, take a few steps back from each corner of the car, and squat. Does the car sit level or is one corner sagging? It's not a common thing to come across a car with a broken spring which would be the cause for the rear to sag, but if it's a front corner sagging, you're looking at a possible bent frame or a tweaked front end. In either case, the car gets an automatic failure.

FLUIDS TO CHECK: OIL

To check the oil, the car must be on level ground for an accurate reading. Pull the dipstick out and wipe it clean with your rag. Reinsert and remove. The oil should be between the high mark and the add-oil mark. Also, notice what color the oil is. The darker it is, the older it is. With your rag handy, get a dab to rub between your fingers. Does it feel gritty?

Grit could be ground up metal or dirt from oil that is long overdue for a change. Either way it's bad news. Dirty oil is a sign of an owner who doesn't take proper care of his car. Light-colored oil (about the color of honey) is oil that has been recently changed. Ask the seller when the oil was changed last and see if his response coincides with what you see. Now would be a good time ask how often the oil was changed.

If they haven't already offered, ask if they can provide you with some sort of maintenance schedule or ledger that they have been religiously following. What you want to see is a schedule where the car's oil was changed regularly every 3,000 miles. Even up to every 5,000 miles is acceptable, but when you get up to six, seven, or 10,000 miles, then you have an engine with excessive wear. So, the more frequent the oil changes, the less wear on the engine and the better off you'll be.

Another thing you want to check is under the oil filler cap. Unscrew it and take a look. If there's a light brown, foamy substance on the underside of the cap, it means water from your cooling system is getting into your engine which could be through a head gasket or cracked block. This is bad news. Likewise oil will be making its way into the cooling system. Keep this in mind when you inspect the radiator. Any coolant getting into the engine or oil getting into the radiator gets an automatic failure.

AUTOMATIC TRANSMISSION

Find the automatic transmission dipstick and pull it out. Some cars have two high and two low marks for when the engine is running and when it is not. Just as long as the fluid registers on the dipstick, we are more concerned with the color and smell of the fluid rather than the level. With your rag nearby, get some on your finger and take a sniff. It should not smell burnt and should be pink in color. If it's brown and burnt smelling, then you are looking at a car that will soon be needing a new transmission. This automatic transmission gets an automatic failure. Walk away.

COOLANT

Make sure the engine is cold by lightly touching the radiator cap. If it's hot, don't try to take it off or you'll be taking a steam bath, which isn't much fun. If it's warm, you can drape your rag over it and turn SLOWLY. If it's cold, no problem. Just push down and turn in the direction the arrow indicates.

Look inside the radiator. The fluid should be a yellowish-green color. If it is brown or rusty in color, then this is a sign of a car overdue for a radiator flush and, hence, a car that is not being properly maintained. If it's clear, the car's cooling system has been drained and refilled with nothing but water, or is leaking and the owner just keeps adding water. In either case, this is a big no-no. New radiators can get pricey. Make a note for your mechanic, and he can give you an estimate later.

Most cars today come with a reservoir tank for the radiator. It is usually a plastic tank with a high and low mark on it. You can easily locate it by following the small hose that comes out from under the radiator cap to the unit. Make sure the fluid is between the marks and of the right color. Also, remember to check for any leaks before and after the test drive.

CHECK AIR FILTER, HOSES, AND BELTS

It's important to check the air cleaner to make sure it is in place. You wouldn't want to buy a car from some fool who has been driving around without one and allowing dust and dirt particles to wreak havoc on the cylinder walls. Plus, the clean or dirty filter will confirm the car's proper or improper maintenance. If the car's filter is in one of those confusing contraptions, leave it for your mechanic to check.

Visually check all hoses you come across on the engine. Even though they're inexpensive and easy enough to replace, you want to make sure they are all in apple pie order. There should be no cracked hoses with duct tape or electrical tape holding them together. Owners who do this are the ones you don't want to buy a car from. If they duct taped a $2.99 hose, you can imagine how long they went between oil changes.

Fan belts, air-conditioning belts, alternator belts, etc., check them all. And before you go putting your hand down there, make sure the keys are not in the ignition and pull the center wire out from the distributor cap. That's that round thing with a bunch of thick wires that come from it and go to each spark plug. Pull the center one.

Using your flashlight, take a peak at the underside of the belt(s). The belt should be tight enough so that it just barely allows you to do this. Check them as much as your point of view will allow. Do the belts look cracked or frayed? If they do, you'll want to have new ones installed. Belts don't cost much, but they can be tricky to replace. Put down $30 per belt on your checklist which will cover labor as well.

THINGS TO LEAK OUT FOR

With your flashlight, check the engine block for oil seepage and leaks. Look all around on both sides. Does it coincide with the amount of miles on the odometer? The less miles on a car, the cleaner the engine should be. An engine with only 60,000 miles on it should have only some minor road grime, but don't freak out if there is some oily grime. As mileage starts to add up, most engines will seep a little oil from around the valve cover or the oil pan, yet it may still be a good running engine with plenty of spunk left in it.

So don't let this scare you, but do be afraid when you see WET oil seepage anywhere on the engine. This could be serious. Check the ground under where the car is parked. If you are in a spot where the car is usually parked, like the garage or driveway, notice how stained the ground is. If the car is parked in the street, then see if you notice any oil stains in their driveway or, if possible, in their garage. An oil stained driveway is more evidence of a car with a leakage problem.

Using your flashlight, look underneath the engine from the front as well as the right and left sides. An oily undercarriage is evidence of oil leaking while driving, and the wind is spraying it back. Look for fresh oil droplets under the engine and transmission. If you see droplets, ask the owner to start up the car (NOT WHILE YOU'RE UNDER THERE) to see if it starts dripping more.

Give the car a few minutes to get the oil circulating. If you notice steady oil dripping while the car is running, there could be a crack in the crankcase, a blown seal, or maybe someone simply forgot to tighten something down last time the car was worked on. Have the owner turn off the engine.

In the latter case, even though tightening something down could be easy enough to fix, you don't know how long the car has been like this or how many times the owner ran the oil down too low. Any car with steady oil dripping receives an automatic failure in my book. Don't take the risk. If there are fresh oil drops, but it doesn't drip while running, then continue with your inspection.

Whether this auto features a standard or automatic transmission, you'll want to have a look at its belly to see if it's leaking any fluid as well. Transmission leaks are not as common as engine oil leaks, but they do occur and, as long as you're under there with a flashlight looking for oil leaks, you may as well inspect the transmission too.

The transmission is bolted to the engine, usually directly behind it but not always. Many of the newer four-cylinder models are set sideways under the hood with a transaxle, making one compact mass of metal.

Shine the light on it and look for anything wet. It should be dry as a bone minus some road dirt. Automatic transmission fluid is pinkish-red, so if it is wet, touch it with your finger and verify that it is automatic transmission fluid and not oil. Vice versa when you are looking for oil leaks. Standard transmissions rarely leak, so make sure it is the transmission you are checking and not the engine. If the transmission is leaking gear oil (which looks like motor oil), let your mechanic make the diagnosis.

Other leaky things to watch for are radiator coolant and hydraulic brake/clutch fluid. Radiator coolant is greenish-yellow in color and mixed with water. If a car hasn't had a radiator flush in a long time, then the color would be closer to a rusty brown. If you see this kind of fluid under the radiator or engine, there could be a leaking water pump or a leaking radiator. Both puppies start in the $200 to $300 range and go up. But don't fail this car yet. Make a note for your mechanic, and he will give you an accurate diagnosis/estimate.

Hydraulic brake/clutch fluid is a clear oil-like substance with a strong smell. By looks, you could confuse it with new oil, but it has that strong odor which is hard to describe. So, next opportunity you have, use your own car, or your friend's if you don't have one, and familiarize yourself with it. Get a rag and find the master cylinder reservoir under the hood. Pop off the cap, get a dab on your finger, and take a whiff. Now you know what brake fluid smells like, and you won't confuse it with oil. By the way, don't get any on your clothes or the paint. It can do damage to both.

If you suspect a car is leaking brake fluid, step down firmly on the brake pedal. If the pedal goes down to the floor, don't drive the car. There is a major leak somewhere, and the brakes won't be working properly. The pedal should go down about halfway and stop. Keep the pressure on for a minute and see if it gives any more. If it does, there is a leak. If it doesn't, it's probably okay. If the brakes seem fine but you found some fluid, make a note and your mechanic can check it out later.

If you come across a car leaking hydraulic clutch fluid, it will either be coming from the master cylinder, which is mounted against the firewall under the hood, or from the slave cylinder that is mounted to the transmission. In the case of a leaking clutch master cylinder, it is possible for the fluid to drip inside the car. It would come down from behind the clutch pedal. Don't fail the car if you detect any leakage. It's not super expensive to replace the clutch master cylinder but, nonetheless, you have discovered more bargaining leverage. Make a note for your mechanic, and he can fill you in later.

CALIFORNIA EMISSIONS

California residents: there should be a sticker on the underside of the hood which declares that the vehicle meets federal AND State of California emission controls. That doesn't mean someone couldn't have later removed some smog control equipment, or the sticker for that matter, but this would be the place to start looking for clues. If the sticker says it meets only federal emission controls, then the car originated from out of state. Look for this sticker when checking out the car.

Another thing to check for is the gas filler tube. Open it up and make sure the inlet hasn't been modified to accept the larger leaded gas nozzle. If it has, then assume regular gas has been run through the engine and the catalytic converter is spent. If this is the case, the car won't pass smog until a new catalytic converter is replaced, which can cost upwards of $300. People have been known to do this in order to save on the cheaper gas at the pumps. If they were that cheap, imagine how often they changed their oil! Give this car an automatic failure.

As long as a car has all the required smog equipment, and the engine is in tune, it should pass the smog inspection with no problem. If a car fails smog with all the required emission equipment, and there's no evidence of tampering, the state has a cap on how much can be charged to correct it. For 1990 and newer vehicles, the cost can't be more than $300, for 1980-89 vehicles, not more than $175--and the cost decreases with age. Cars with repair estimates over the caps get waivered and, hence, a smog certificate.

THE TAIL PIPE

A car's tail pipe is one of the best ways to tell how an engine is running. Look inside the tail pipe and check the color. A normal running engine should be light gray to light brown. If the tail pipe isn't hot, run your finger around inside. Black sooty wet deposits indicate too rich a mixture, while black oily deposits mean it's burning oil. If it looks white and glazed, the engine is running too hot--the timing could be off. If the color is anything but light gray to light brown, make a note for your mechanic.

CHECK THE GLASS

Glass is an easy detail to overlook. Make sure you check the windows carefully for small cracks or chips that may later turn into big cracks and render its replacement. The windshield is the one most subject to nicks and chips from road pebbles. If you come across a cracked window, you'll need to call an auto glass shop for a quote. The cost of a new windshield and installation can get pretty pricey. Pay particular attention.

ABOUT SUNROOFS

I have this to say about sunroofs--know the difference between factory (original) and custom. If you're looking at a car with a factory sunroof, then you're looking at something that adds value to the car. However, a custom sunroof that some high school kid bought at the auto parts store and installed himself, or even one that was professionally installed by John Doe's Sunroofs, can actually hurt the value of a car.

Nine times out of ten custom sunroofs leak. Nine times out of ten potential used car buyers are turned off when they see a car with a custom sunroof. Most kids think they're cool, but when they pay hundreds to get one installed, not only are they out the initial cost, they are out hundreds more when they try to resell. Avoid cars with custom sunroofs. They're bad news.

As for factory sunroofs, whether power or manual, check the full range of movement and see that it seats properly. Check around the inside for evidence of leakage such as stained headliner or stained seats.

INTERIOR

You will also want to visually check out the interior. The front seats, the back seats, the headliner, the carpet, everything should look in order. Is the dash cracked? They are expensive to replace, so you can either live with it or do what I do and cover it up with a dash saver. They cost about 80 bucks. Put it down on your checklist.

Even though the seller told you the mileage over the phone, check it now. I've had plenty of people tell me they have 60,000 miles on their car and when I look it reads 69,900 miles. This is an easy way for people to exaggerate. What's another 9,900 miles? Keep in mind that if they exaggerate about the mileage, they'll be exaggerating about everything else. Believe what they say accordingly.

Check to see if the owner's manual is in the glove box. If it's not, ask if they have it. It's important to have the owner's manual so you can acquaint yourself with the car and learn about the maintenance schedule, oil recommendations, etc. If they don't have one, then put down $25.00 for the cost of a replacement on your checklist.

How does the driver's seat look? This will be the seat with the most wear. Is it torn or cracked? You can either live with it or do the seat-cover thing. Put it down on your checklist.

Keep in mind while you're looking at all this, everything should be in agreement with the odometer. If the car has 60,000 miles on it, then the interior should look like a car that has been driven 60,000 miles, not 160,000. If there seems to be extreme wear, like worn pedal pads on a low mileage car, then suspect odometer tampering. If the odometer doesn't run over 100,000 miles, then it could have turned over. Ask the seller. If he claims that it has not turned over, but your eyes tell you differently, then believe your eyes and assume that they are not telling the truth.

Check each of the crank-up windows and make sure they are working properly. If the car has power windows, then check each window from the master control and at each door as well. And don't be embarrassed about it. You wouldn't want to sell your car to someone without him first checking everything, would you? Make sure all doors lock and unlock manually and with the key. Ditto for power door locks.

Don't forget to check the heater in the summer and the air-conditioner in the winter. Also check the following: emergency brakes, horn, headlights (both high and low beam), turn signals, four-ways, brake lights, back-up lights, dome light, dash lights, windshield washer and wipers, and the radio. If the car is a convertible, whether it's manual or power, you'll want to check this too. Check any other power options, such as power seats, antenna, tilt steering, etc., and make notes accordingly.

Remember, if the car has something not working right, like a power window, you'll need to call the dealer to get a phone estimate for what the MAXIMUM cost would be to fix it. Make sure you do this before you make an offer to purchase. Don't disregard something that the seller may claim as trivial. You may be in shock when you find out what a new power window unit costs for a car these days.

LUGGAGE COMPARTMENT

Use the remote release to open the trunk if the car offers one. Open it with the key as well. Unless this is a truck, the spare tire is usually below the trunk matting. There should also be a jack, lug wrench, and jack handle. Is anything missing? Put it on your checklist and get prices from the dealer later. Is the spare tire a real one, or is it one of those dummy tires? I think they call them dummy tires because whoever came up with the bright idea is a big dummy.

Consider the following: You sell real estate and are enroute to a nearby town to close a six-figure deal on a house. Suddenly you have a blow out. Now, if you have a real spare, you can still make it, but if you have a dummy tire, guess what? That's right, you're hating it. You can't drive at freeway speeds safely with a dummy tire on your car. So you can forget about closing that real estate deal. Right now you have to go find a tire shop and get a new tire installed. Meanwhile, six-figure-earning decision-makers in the auto industry are busy designing their next "great" money-saving idea. The moral of the story? What's good for the auto industry isn't always good for the people.

FLOOD CARS

In times of flooding, opportunists will buy up dozens of water-damaged vehicles for next to nothing, clean them up, get them running, and ship them to another region of the country. These flood cars are to be avoided at all costs. Water will get into sealed compartments and promote rust while wreaking havoc on the car's entire electrical system via corrosion. The worst part is, the car will appear fine while these problems lie just around the corner.

The easiest way to detect a flood car is with your nose. Sniff around the interior for musty mildew. Check underneath the carpeting, floor mats, seats, and in the trunk compartment for silt and rust. Look for a water line on the interior and exterior of the car. Moisture trapped in the headlights or in the dash panel are also warning flags of a flood car. Any suspected flood car receives an automatic failure.

THE EIGHT GOLDEN RULES OF CHECKING OUT THE BEAST

1) Always show up early
2) Always look at a car in daylight
3) Always bring a flashlight
4) Know how to check for hidden body damage and rust
5) Always check inside the tail pipe
6) Arrange it so you be will checking out a cold engine
7) Thoroughly inspect the interior
8) Never be in a hurry to buy a used car

CHAPTER 4:

THE TEST DRIVE

The car has passed the body/rust inspection and doesn't seem to have a serious oil leak. You have also checked out all the previously mentioned steps and have made your notes accordingly. Now you are ready for the test drive. If you are in an unfamiliar area, you will want to have the owner direct you to a quiet side street, preferably a dead end, as well as a freeway or open road where you can cruise up to 60 mph or so.

LISTEN WITH YOUR EARS

When you do the test drive you will be listening for sounds. You will listen to the engine perform, the transmission shift, and the tires roll. What are you listening for? Anything that doesn't sound right. So, if at all possible, try to test drive the car without the owner. This way you can test drive the car without the seller right next to you babbling away about this and that and drawing your attention away from the car's performance. Most likely, though, sellers will insist on coming along, and you really can't blame them. They don't know who you are and may be worried about you not coming back at all.

Before driving the car, start the engine with the hood still up. You want to listen to the engine. If the engine was dead cold, it should idle high, indicating that the choke is on. After a minute or two, a light tap on the accelerator should slow the engine down to normal idle speed. This should be around 800 rpms for those cars with tachometers. If the engine was already warm, the engine should idle at a low speed. Try to make a point to look at a car with a cold engine. If possible, first thing in the morning would be the optimum time.

Listen to the valves. They make a clickety-click-click-clickety-click-click sound that comes from the top of the engine. Does the clickety-click-click sound almost obnoxious, indicating loose valves? Do all the clickety-click-clicks sound equal or does one sound different from the others, indicating one loose valve?

Before you hang your head over the engine to listen, remember there are moving parts. The spinning fan blade can yank the hair right out of your head or grab your loose necktie and strangle you to death. PAY ATTENTION!

Of course, I don't expect someone with no experience to decipher what they hear, but at least you can look like you know what you're doing, which is important in front of sellers. Remember, they don't know who your are or what your background is.

Are there any other sounds that draw your attention? Do you hear a deep popping sound coming from the side or behind the engine? This could be an exhaust leak. The exhaust manifold may need some tightening down or it could be warped and in need of a new one. A new exhaust manifold is a pricey part that is difficult to replace. Your mechanic can diagnose it.

Another strange sound you may hear is an ear-piercing screech coming from the front of the engine. Sometimes it will go away once the engine is warm and sometimes it won't. The screeching usually comes from a rapidly wearing fan belt or air-conditioning belt that has its pulleys out of alignment. Cars with this problem go through a lot of belts. Again, your mechanic can diagnose it. Although it sounds like hell, it could be simple to fix and a great excuse to get the price lower.

Having test driven many cars, I have seen a lot of the same tactics. The seller talks nonstop and distracts you from your test drive. For talkative sellers, ask them nicely to be quiet so that you may listen to the engine perform. When they turn on their stereo and start bragging how they paid $1,000 for it, do what I do. Reply with, "Why don't you pull the stereo system and we'll knock $1,000 off the price?" This shuts them up really quick, every time.

CHECK THE BRAKES

You want a quiet or dead-end street to test the brakes. On a straight and level road, with no one in sight behind you, get the car up to about 30 mph. You don't want to slam on the brakes to lock them up, but you do want to hit the brakes firmly to see how well the car stops. A verbal warning to your passengers before you do this is always nice.

The pedal should feel solid without the use of extreme force. Of course, if the car has power brakes, the pedal will be much more sensitive and need less pressure. Most importantly, the car should not pull to the left or to the right. It should brake evenly. If you thought you felt a tug to one side try it again, but this time use less force and let the steering wheel slip loosely through your fingers so the car goes the direction it wants.

Of course, I don't have to remind you to be safe about this and tell you to double check for any cars in sight behind you, but I will anyway. DO IT! And be careful when you hit the brakes and let the wheel go loose. You don't want to go crashing into a parked car and have a real mess on your hands. Do this test on a road that has no traffic and allows plenty of maneuvering space.

If the car pulls to one side, straighten the car out and continue with your inspection. You have just discovered that either the brakes are out of adjustment or the car needs new brakes, period. Make a note, or, better yet, have your assistant make a note because you're still driving.

Cars that pull to one side when you brake are extremely dangerous on wet roads. If you hit the brakes hard on a wet surface, you will go into a skid. So uneven braking is something you want to get fixed pronto. Your mechanic can diagnose the problem and give you an estimate at the same time.

ABOUT BRAKE NOISES

It's a common thing for disc breaks to squeak. Sometimes they squeak when you apply the brakes and sometimes they squeak when you drive. It doesn't necessarily mean that the car needs a brake job. Most new brakes squeak until they're broken in. Just make sure you mention it to your mechanic when you bring it in. He can easily check the brake pads and discs and report to you exactly how much life is left on them.

However, there is a brake noise you should be wary of. If you apply the brakes and hear a soft grinding noise which can sometimes be felt through the brake pedal, it's a sure sign of brake pads that are spent. Not only is the car unsafe to drive, the disc rotor is being damaged every time you apply the brakes. My advice here is to turn the car around and carefully head back. The car needs new brakes immediately and you don't want to test drive it until the car is safe. If the brakes check out, continue.

CHECK THE ALIGNMENT

While still out on those straight level roads, you can test the front-end alignment. Again, do this test on a straight and level surface where there isn't any traffic. Going about 35 mph or so, let the steering wheel slip freely through your hands. If the road is straight and level, the car should go straight as well. If the car wants to go to the right or left, grab the wheel, straighten it out and try it again. Did it do it again in the same direction? It could be just uneven tire pressure, but more than likely, the car needs a front-end alignment. Remember, if it pulls to one side only when the brakes are applied then it's a brake problem.

Also, if you notice the steering wheel shimmying (vibrating abnormally) at any certain speed during the test drive, then that's a sure sign of an alignment problem. Alignment can cost anywhere from $40 to $400 depending on what may need replacing. But don't let an alignment problem stop your inspection. Make a note on your checklist and make sure you mention it to your mechanic before he inspects it. He should be able to give you an accurate estimate, which you will, of course, use for bargaining leverage.

CHECK THE TRANSMISSION

While still on one of those quiet roads, you want to check reverse. If you are in a hilly area, backing up the slope is preferred. Make sure you can see clearly behind you for a great distance. Put the car in reverse and back up slowly at first. You should have the windows down to listen for any noises. The car should back up smoothly.

If you are test driving a car with a standard transmission, step on the accelerator to increase the speed and then abruptly let off the gas. Try it again. Everything working okay? What you're trying to detect is whether the transmission pops out of reverse and into neutral (more on this shortly). If it didn't, then continue on with your inspection.

For standard transmissions, it shouldn't be difficult to find a gear, nor should it be difficult to put into a gear. The stick shift should move in and out of each gear easily. Difficulty shifting into gear is usually a sign of a worn clutch not doing its job. Unless you'd rather not hassle with getting a new clutch installed, continue with your inspection. Depending on the model, a new clutch assembly can be anywhere from $200 to $500. If your mechanic verifies that the car will need a new clutch, have him give you an estimate and use this amount as more bargaining leverage.

Stick shifters that pop out of gear while driving indicate worn teeth in the gear box which means you will need a costly overhaul or a new transmission altogether. In either case, it's an automatic failure. Steer clear of cars that pop out of gear when you drive them. Even if you could replace the transmission for $500, worn-out transmissions go hand in hand with worn-out engines. Chances are you will be needing some serious engine work soon.

For automatic tramsmissions, pay attention to how it shifts for the rest of the test drive. It should be smooth and sure, not clunky or moving in and out of speeds like it can't decide where it wants to be.

Also, whether the car is standard or automatic, any metal-to-metal grinding noises coming from the transmission should get an automatic failure from you. Drive it carefully back to the owner's house and politely leave.

THE OPEN ROAD

Next, drive the car to a freeway or open road where you can go a comfortable 60 mph. On the way to the freeway, you want to notice how the car handles around corners. It should hug the road smoothly without shimmying. Also on the way there, you are still listening for sounds and paying attention to the engine's performance. The engine and transmission should work together, accelerating and shifting smoothly, with confidence.

As you enter the freeway, don't be afraid to step on the gas, but don't be abusive either. You want to see exactly how much power this engine has to offer and how well the transmission shifts from one gear to the next. When you get up to 50 mph or so, keep it steady for a moment. If the road isn't crowded, try the alignment test again. Does it hold true or does it pull to the right or left?

At 50 mph, imagine you are following a slowpoke on a two-lane highway and you need to pass him quickly. With no one if front of you, step down on the gas to see what kind of passing power the engine has. Is the engine very responsive or does it lag for a moment before kicking in? A responsive engine is what we like to see, but a hesitation at 50 mph usually means one of three things: Either there's a problem with carburetion/injection, or a problem with the automatic transmission taking too long to shift into the right gear (standard drivers--make sure you are in the right gear), or that's just the way the car is and you have to live with it. Most of the time it's the latter case. Make sure you remember to make a note on your checklist to mention this to your mechanic later.

When you return from your test drive, check again with your flashlight under the hood and under the car for anything leaking. Most fluid leaks become more severe once the engine is hot.

ABOUT RECEIPTS

Don't be shy about asking for them. If someone claims they have kept all their receipts and informs you that a new clutch was installed last month, don't believe them until you verify the receipt yourself. PEOPLE WILL LIE ABOUT WORK DONE TO THEIR CAR! They have a good motive. They're trying to sell you a car.

Plenty of times I have called on a receipt that sellers have claimed possession of and they were unable to produce it. Somehow the one from last month's clutch job mysteriously disappeared! When this happens, their claim of repair loses validity. These people are playing with you. People who save all their receipts don't lose the big ones from last month.

When you do look at a receipt, make sure it belongs to the car that the owner claims. Check the date, year, make, and model, and somewhere on there will be the license plate number. Also, the mileage of the car at the time of repair should be logged in there as well. All this information should coincide with what the seller is saying about his car.

Pay particular attention to the mileage. This is where you can catch evidence of odometer tampering. Is the amount currently on the car more than what was logged on the receipt in the past? Keep in mind that many vehicle odometers won't go over 100,000 miles, which means they will turn over and start again. So if the owner claims that the 58,000 miles currently on the odometer is the actual mileage and you notice 95,000 miles on a three-year-old receipt, you know the odometer has either been tampered with or the car has 158,000 miles on it. Watch out for this.

THE CHARACTER THING

How do you drive your car? Do you drive it hard (quick accelerations and heavy braking) or do you generally take it easy? Do you change the oil every 3,000 miles or whenever you get around to it? Do you wash and clean your car regularly or do you tend to let it go? Do you have the major services performed on schedule as the owner's manual states, or do you stretch as far as you can?

This is all part of the character thing. You know how you treat your car, and when looking at a used auto you need to try to figure out what kind of person the seller is and how he treated his car. Was he the kind who took it easy or drove it hard? Is he retired or is he eighteen years old? Is his house and yard neat in appearance or does it have kids toys strewn about and peeling paint on the house?

So remember, the whole time you're checking out a used car you're also checking out the seller. What kind of person is he or she? You need to make a character judgement in twenty minutes. Find out about this person through observation and small talk. You can get a feel for what kind of driver he is and how well he cared for his car.

People take care of their cars the same way they take care of their houses and yards. It may sound silly, but it's true. I want to tell you a story, and I'll keep it short. Being the camper and outdoor enthusiast that I am, I decided I was going to buy a camper. I found one advertised that was just around the corner, so I went over to have a look. While I was knocking on the solid oak front door, I noticed badly peeling varnish. I mean, it looked horrible and stood out like a sore thumb.

A middle-aged gentleman opened the door and invited me in. His camper was in the backyard, and he would lead me through his house to get there. As soon as I stepped inside there was a staircase that went up to the left. On every step there were boxes and stuff stacked up to where there was just barely enough room to pass by. The first thing that entered my mind was that they must be in the middle of moving.

Stepping over kids' toys on the way to the living room, we passed the open kitchen area. Every counter top was covered with magazines, newspapers and Lord knows what else. Through the living room you had to watch your step for more kids' toys and junk that lined the floor. The areas of carpeting that were exposed looked so matted, I figured it hadn't been vacuumed in years.

Through a dirty sliding glass door and by a filthy pool surrounded by broken pool toys was where he had his camper set up.

"It's just been sitting here for two years as the kids' play room," he said as the knot in my stomach tightened. I poked my nose inside and saw things broken and missing, and junk all over the place. The camper was so filthy dirty inside and out, I was disgusted. And it takes a lot to disgust me. I used my "just-started-looking" excuse and high-tailed it out of there.

With that said, it's easy to see the relation here. Sometimes it's not that obvious, and you need to look a little closer to find those telltale signs that reveal the type of character you're dealing with. If you're buying a car from an owner whose house and yard is neat and tidy, you have reason to feel good about the car. You are buying from an owner who takes pride in ownership.

However, if the seller's garage and yard look like a war zone, you have reason to be uneasy even if his auto checks out by your mechanic. You'll never know what sins have been committed until later. The moral of the story? It pays to be observant.

A WASTE OF TIME AND MONEY?

Some of you may think that going to a mechanic is a waste of your time and money, especially if you just thoroughly checked out the car yourself. On the other hand, some of you may wonder why bother with checking it over yourself when you can have a mechanic do it more competently. I would like to answer both of these up front.

First of all, not even a mechanic knows for sure what condition an engine is in until he has compression tested it and test driven it. You could buy a car that seems to be running well, but it may really need a valve job or it could have a cylinder with a broken ring or it may need the top-end completely rebuilt. In any case, it will cost you plenty to get it corrected. So if you spend 50 bucks and have a mechanic report this, don't think of it as 50 dollars down the drain.

You just saved yourself a lot of money and headaches. This is money well spent.

As far as not inspecting the car yourself and relying totally on the mechanic, you'll be paying out a lot of money in mechanic's fees when cars fail inspection on simple things you could have caught yourself.

This is why you should learn how to thoroughly inspect a car. You're weeding out the undesirables and bringing only the ones that passed your rigorous inspection to the mechanic. And once the car has passed his inspection, you'll own a car that will allow you to sleep peacefully at night.

GOING TO YOUR MECHANIC

Now that you have found a car that has passed every test and inspection listed above, the next step is to have it inspected by your mechanic. Tell the seller you are interested in buying the car, but first wish to have it looked at by your mechanic at your own expense. Most people won't object to this, especially when they know their car is in fine shape.

If, for any reason, the seller won't allow you to do this, tell him you're sorry you couldn't do business and walk away. Don't let him make up excuses why he can't get the time to do it. If he wants to sell his car, he will have to make time. Having a car checked over is a common practice, so don't let him talk you out of it. Either he lets you have your mechanic check it out or the deal's off--period.

Why do I feel strongly about this? Because there are plenty of people selling used cars with hidden defects who will tell you otherwise... "Ah you don't need no mechanic to look at this, it runs perfect. Besides, I'm very busy with my work and don't have time and da da-da da-da..." No matter how sincere, trust no one.

People who do this usually have something to hide. If something is wrong with his car, he knows your mechanic will catch it, thus keeping him from selling it to you. So be especially wary of anyone trying to talk you out of seeing your mechanic. Either he succumbs to your request or you walk. It's that simple.

Most of the time, people won't mind having their cars inspected. What you need to do is call your mechanic as soon as possible to schedule an appointment when it's convenient for the seller to meet you at your mechanic's shop. Your mechanic should spend a good hour checking things out. This is the time to give him that list of notes you made about things in question, such as brake noises, oil seepage, etc.

He should do a compression test, battery and charging test, frame inspection, fluid leakage inspection, alignment and suspension check, brake inspection, and test drive the car for engine and transmission performance. When it's all said and done, he should report to you in private about his findings.

In most cases, the car will have several less serious things wrong that will start adding up. He will tell you about the current problems as well as the problems that are just around the corner. It may need front brakes soon and tires all the way around, etc. Your mechanic can give you accurate estimates on repairs; and from his report you can make any necessary adjustments to your proposed offer.

Your mechanic may ask you what the selling price is and advise you on what to offer. This may be good advice but, remember, that's his opinion. Don't let this keep you from making an offer lower than what the mechanic thinks is a fair price. Even though what you had in mind may seem like a low-pitch offer, you can back it up with the mechanic's report, which gives you muscle to bargain with.

In other words, you're not someone B.S.'ing the sellers about something you think may be wrong. You have it in writing by a certified mechanic which the sellers can see for themselves. When they find problems with their car that they didn't know about before, they usually become more flexible in their price. Who knows, they may even succumb to your first offer, which would recoup that $50 mechanic's bill many times over.

Remember, if your mechanic tells you right off the bat there's something seriously wrong and advises you that the car is a bad buy, don't get frustrated thinking you just threw away 50 bucks. In actuality, you saved hundreds or maybe even thousands by dodging a car with a serious problem. In addition, you just gained some valuable experience that can be applied when looking at your next car.

DOUBLE CHECK FOR RECALLS

Between the time you find a car and the time you hand over the cash, you should check to see if the car has had any recalls and, if so, whether they were corrected. A good time to do this would be when you are waiting for your mechanic to complete his inspection.

This can be easily done with one phone call to the respective dealership for the car you're considering. You will need the Vehicle's Indentification Number, so copy it down before you call. Within a matter of minutes, the service department will give you the status of that specific car. You will know immediately whether or not the car has a recall that needs to be addressed.

Even though recall problems are repaired free by the manufacturer, there is the inconvenience of having to take time out of your busy day to get it corrected. This could be used as another excuse to lower the price a little more. Consider using it for additional bargaining leverage.

THE SIX GOLDEN RULES OF THE TEST DRIVE

1) Listen for anything that doesn't sound right
2) Ask for, and check, all receipts
3) Observe the owner's characteristics
4) Take the car to your mechanic
5) Check the recall history
6) Never be in a hurry to buy a used car

CHAPTER 5:

NEGOTIATING

Haggling can be the thrill of the kill for some and the agony of the purchase for others. Wherever you place yourself in the spectrum, remember this: Smart negotiating can save you hundreds of dollars right off the bat. There's nothing to be bashful about or ashamed of. It's your hard-earned money. Make the seller earn it.

If you are one of those who is not comfortable with negotiating, keep in mind that the people with whom you are dealing with may not be comfortable with it either. By playing tough, you can capitalize on their fear of haggling and create an edge for yourself without even trying hard.

Negotiating with a private party will occur in three phases. In the first phase, you will prenegotiate or precondition the seller to lower his price.

In the second phase, you will negotiate with the seller and agree upon a price with the assumption that your mechanic does not find anything wrong. If, however, your mechanic does find a problem(s) that you missed, this will open the door for further negotiations.

The final phase, obviously, is renegotiating after your mechanic has looked the car over and caught a few minor things that you were not aware of. You add up the total estimate for repairs and approach the seller with your new offer based on the additional findings.

PHASE 1: PRECONDITIONING

The preconditioning phase begins with the phone call when you ask, "How much are you asking for it?" You will ask this same question at least two more times: once during the visual inspection and once during or immediately following the test drive.

When calling on an ad, even if the price is stated clearly in bold letters, ask the question anyway. This works best after a question you had just asked drew a negative response about the car. For example, if you ask, "How many miles are on it?" and their answer reveals high mileage, or you ask, "What shape is the body in?" and their answer reveals a scratch on the hood, this would be the perfect time to ask "How much are you asking for it?"

This preconditions sellers to lower their price, which they may do immediately over the phone. When sellers compensate you over the phone for a fault with their car, they set the stage for further deductions for any additional faults you may find during your inspection. If they don't lower the price over the phone, then they should let you know in their answer that they will compensate you for their car's faults. They will most likely tell you right out that their price is negotiable or that they are accepting offers, etc.

During your visual inspection, touch every little flaw on the car, making sure the seller sees you. Then go back and touch the biggest visual flaw the car has and ask again, "How much are you asking for this car?" as if you couldn't believe they wanted so much. The seller may lower his price again just to keep you interested. Even if it's only a little, it puts you that much closer to making a deal.

For the test drive segment, again, find another major flaw related to the mechanics of the car. Is the car out of alignment and pulling to one side? Does the car need a new muffler? Mention the problem(s) to the seller.

To keep from sounding like a broken record when you ask the third time, say, "I'm sorry, but I've called on so many cars this past week; how much did you say you were asking for this car?" Boom. You have just informed the seller that you are a serious buyer who is not afraid to shop around. He knows that, if he is to sell his car, he better lower his price a little more.

Another form of preconditioning works when you have called and left a message on a seller's recorder. Let's say the car you called on was an '89 model advertised in the classifieds for $3,500. When he calls back you deliberately say "I'm sorry, but I have called on a bunch of cars today. Was yours the '89 selling for $3,000?" Now the seller believes there is another car on the market, the same year as his, selling for $500 less. He realizes he will have to bargain if he wants to sell you his car. He may respond with, "No, mine was for $3,500, but the price is negotiable." Bingo! This translates to "No, mine was for $3,500, but I'd probably take $3,000 for it." You just got $500 dollars knocked off the price without even looking at the car yet. That's a sizeable reduction. Preconditioning really works. Try it.

PHASE 2: NEGOTIATING BEFORE THE MECHANIC'S INSPECTION

Preconditioning is a way to get the seller to lower the price or prepare him to lower the price before you make your offer. At the beginning of the second negotiation phase you want to continue with this momentum of getting the seller to come down as low as possible. This will create an edge for you by cutting the spread between his asking price and your target purchase price without you having yet made an offer.

As for deciding on your target purchase price, that's something you consider only after inspecting and test driving the car. You must decide what would be the most you'd be willing to fork over for this particular car (with the assumption that your mechanic doesn't find any significant flaws, of course) and do your best to get the seller to meet you there. When you reach the final phase of negotiation, you may need to readjust your target purchase price when the mechanic informs you of problems that you were unaware of.

Before submitting your offer, don't get too greedy and attempt to suck the seller bone dry by making an offer way below the asking price, especially if he didn't seem too receptive during preconditioning. Save the bone-sucking for the final phase. Besides, at this point he may take it as an insult and tell you to take a walk.

So how do you know where to start with your first offer? Judging by the responses you received during the preconditioning phase, you should have a good idea of how open the seller is to a low-pitch offer. Did he appear rigid or receptive to lower offers? Before you submit any offer, there are still more things to consider:

• **The condition and price of the car** - Is the car in near perfect condition and priced at fair market value, or is there a dent in the fender and the price seems high? If the car is in excellent shape and priced fairly, then be more conservative in your offer. But when a car has several minor problems and seems overpriced, by all means, make that low offer.

• **Feel the seller out** - Ask why he is selling the car and if anyone else has looked at it yet. Even though you asked the same questions over the phone, ask him again to see if the answers vary. Is he moving or in need of money for other reasons? Has no one else looked at it, and his phone hasn't been ringing? Do you detect a bit of desperation in his voice? If this is the case, don't hesitate to make that low pitch offer.

• **The car's immediate needs** - Does the car need immediate repair work, i.e., brakes, tires, paint, etc., that the seller told you about or that you discovered on your own? The more immediate needs the car has, the more liberal you can be with your low offer.

After carefully weighing all these considerations, tell the seller you are interested in buying the car (that is, if you still are), but have a problem with the price. Ask what his bottom price is and see what kind of response you get. Whatever price he comes up with, don't accept it as written in stone. Chances are he will go lower, but is just testing the negotiation waters with you.

Okay, enough of all this jibber-jabber. It's example time. Let's say you were looking at a car that was advertised for $5,900. After inspecting and test driving the car, the most you'd be willing to pay is an even $5,000. You came to this conclusion because the mileage is a little high, it will be needing new tires soon, and the past months of studying the market tells you the asking price of $5,900 is inflated.

During the preconditioning phase, the seller knocks off $300 for the flaws you point out, which puts you $600 away from your target price. You tell the seller you are very interested, but have a problem with the price. You then press him for his bottom price and he says he couldn't let it go for anything less than $5,300. With your target price of $5,000 in mind, you would want to offer $4,800, which gives you $200 in bargaining leeway to come up to your price.

Your offer, by the way, is made with the understanding that your mechanic won't find any problems. If he does, then you will be allowed to renegotiate a new sale price for the car. It's always wise to make this crystal clear to the seller before you take the car to your mechanic. This will prevent any misunderstandings when you begin renegotiating and is also another great way to precondition the seller for the possibility of a lower price.

The seller says no to $4,800 and sticks to his $5,300 offer. You then remind him of all that is wrong with the car and the fact that you have several other cars on your list you have yet to look at. Tell him you really want to make this work between you, but he will have to do better than that. The seller goes another $50, making it $5,250. You counter offer $4,850, matching his $50. You are now $400 apart and $250 from your target price.

This would be a good time to change the subject and compliment the seller in some way about his car, home, child, etc. Talk a little bit and ease the tension between you. Some good buttering up can help melt his price some more. Tell the seller how well he cared for his car and how you appreciate people like him who take care of their things. Tell him how you are the same way with your own vehicles and that his car will be well cared for if you were to buy it. Some people get attached to their cars, like pets, and would rather see them go to a good home. Hey, it never hurts to try.

Getting back on the negotiation track, tell him that although the car isn't your favorite color, you are ready to leave a deposit if you can just agree on a price. Remind him how the final payment will be all cash. Coax him. "$4,850. What do you say?" The seller finally budges to $5,200. You then go for broke with your take-it-or-leave-it offer. You tell him this is it; your budget only allowed for $4,800, but you can borrow the rest from a friend to pay an even $5,000 for his car. Be firm. Tell him that's it, take it or leave it. The seller hesitates, scratches his head, hems and haws, and then tries to get you to split the difference and meet at $5,100. You stand firm and say no.

Now, at this point, a hundred dollars above your target price is pretty darn good and if the seller doesn't go for it, you should consider taking it for $5,100. Remember, you will have another chance to get this price lower after your mechanic's inspection. But for the sake of negotiation, and saving money, you are ready to challenge his offer just to see if he really is at his bottom.

If, after further coaxing, the seller still refuses to accept $5,000, ask him if he's sure and remind him of the three other cars on your list you have yet to look at. Don't be afraid to walk away to call his bluff. If he doesn't give in to $5,000, you can always turn around and reconsider, taking the car for $5,100. Chances are, though, he won't let you go and will succumb to your offer. Now the car is yours for $5,000 and you still have an opportunity to get it for a lower price when your mechanic finds a few things wrong that you missed.

A deposit of $100 should be sufficient to have the seller take the car off the market for the day or two you need to get it to your mechanic. Make sure you get a receipt that states that the deposit is refundable should the deal fall through. If the seller will allow it, write a check for the deposit with the mention that the balance will be paid in cash. This way, if the deal falls through and the seller tries to pull a shenanigan, your check is proof of your deposit and you can put a stop-payment on the check if neccessary.

PHASE 3: NEGOTIATING AFTER THE MECHANIC'S INSPECTION

Now, considering it takes a day or two to get an appointment with your mechanic, time has passed since you negotiated to $5,000 with the seller. By now the seller has gotten comfortable with selling his car for $5,000 and is probably excited about getting paid and moving on with his life. When the seller meets you at your mechanic's shop motivated to sell his car, the odds are in your favor of getting his price down a little more.

After the mechanic has inspected the car and consulted privately with you on some new faults that will need attention, have him write up an estimate for everything that needs to be done. For our example's sake, let's say your mechanic found that the car is due for a front brake job, and both axle boots are torn and in need of replacement. His estimate for the work is $250, not including tax.

Approach the seller with your mechanic's report in hand and let him read the bad news. Be gentle, but firm, and give him an option. Either he pays to have the repairs corrected or you deduct the amount from the $5,000 and take the car right now for $4,750. If the seller objects, claiming that he has already come down enough to absorb that, remind him that the price you had agreed on before was under the assumption that there wasn't anything else wrong with the car. Now you have a report that shows axle boots and brake work is needed. In most cases, the seller will give in, but not always.

If the seller happens to be the home mechanic type and claims he can do it himself or has a friend that will do it cheap, tell him that's fine, but once that the car has been repaired you will want to bring it back to your mechanic to make sure the repairs were indeed performed and performed correctly (your mechanic should inspect the questioned repairs for free).

If the seller does not have this option, he would be smart to take your offer of $4,750 rather than having the repairs done by his or your mechanic. Not only will he still get paid today, he won't have the hassle of having to make an appointment and waiting days until the car is ready to sell. Plus, it's not uncommon for unforeseen problems to crop up during repairs which can inflate the estimate significantly. Also, tax wasn't included in the $250 estimate. Mention all this to him and get him thinking how he should take the money and run.

If the seller doesn't want to do either, because he feels he has already come down enough to absorb these additional costs, bargain with him on the $250 estimate. If he isn't willing to knock off the $250, what would he be willing to take off the price in order to save the deal?

Remind the seller about the brake job that needs to be done and two axle boots which are in need of replacement, neither of which you knew about before. Had you known, you would have never agreed on the $5,000 price tag. If the seller still doesn't want to budge, pick the most expensive of the two repairs and tell him that if he compensates you for the cost of that one repair, you will pay for the rest on your own. This will usually get him to act.

However, if he still won't move, don't be afraid to challenge him again. He may be bluffing. Be prepared to shake his hand and tell him how sorry you are you couldn't make this work. After getting your deposit refunded, go back into your mechanic's office and chew the fat with him a minute or two to give the seller some time to change his mind, then walk slowly for your car. If the seller hasn't approached you by the time you have gotten inside your car and put the key in the ignition, then he really is at his bottom.

Now you have to decide if you want to pay $5,000 plus the $250 in repairs (and possibly more) for this car or keep looking. If $5,250 is still well within your budget, you may want to reconsider and grab the seller before he leaves. If, however, your budget is tight and there are more cars on your list to check out, keep looking.

The above example is just that, an example. Every situation is different. If the seller was firm in his price you probably won't get too far in the first or second phase of negotiations. Phase three is where you'll likely gain some ground with a mechanic's report revealing problems in need of attention. If the seller was unaware of these problems, he will likely compensate you. The most important thing to remember is to exercise your negotiation power through each of the three steps and, in the end, you will come out the winner.

EMOTION CONTROL

Buying a used car can get very emotional and it's extremely important to hide your emotions when negotiating. This isn't always easy to do. Consider the following: You've looked at six cars in the past month. Three were junk and two others you had checked out by your mechanic failed because of hidden body damage. With the last car you called about you were certain you had finally found your car, but someone else swooped in and bought it before you even had a chance to look at it.

At this point, you are down a $100 in mechanic's fees, your frustration level is high, and your patience is worn thin. You need to find a car. Finally, you come across the perfect car. It has all the right features, it runs excellent and checks out with your mechanic, and it's even your favorite color. You are happy as a lark.

Do you know what happens when the seller sees your face beaming while you're doing cartwheels of joy? Suddenly he gets real firm in his price. He knows he has a buyer who wants his car bad, and is unlikely to budge in price. If you want to get anywhere with the seller at the negotiation table, then your emotions have to be 180 degrees from this. You have to be deadpan.

Remember, the seller will be observing you as well. When you're checking out the car you must act like you're not impressed with it. Even though inside you're screaming with joy, on the surface you must convince the seller that you're not really interested that much. This keeps the seller guessing as to whether you will even make an offer and he will remain much more flexible when it is time to haggle. It's the reverse-psychology thing. Think like a poker player who's just been dealt an ace-high full-house. You wouldn't want to give yourself away, would you?

Plenty of times I have looked at cars that were reasonably priced where I would have gladly paid the full amount, but instead I bought them for hundreds less. Even though I was willing to pay what they were asking, I would still make a lower offer. If they say no then I make another offer closer to their price. What's the worst that could happen? They don't budge, and you pay full price. But nine times out of ten they will bend a little, if not a lot. And when they do, you have recouped that money spent on mechanic's fees, giving you even more reason to be happy as a lark.

OTHER NEGOTIATION TIPS

Earlier I had mentioned briefly about prices that are followed by the word "firm." This means that the seller doesn't want to budge in price. However, DON'T LET IT KEEP YOU FROM TRYING. For some people, "firm" simply means they want to get close to their asking price. This could be a couple of hundred dollars less.

Again, every situation is different. Feel the person out. Has the car been for sale very long? Has anyone looked at it before you? The seller may realize the price is too high from the lack of interest in it. You'd be surprised how many times I bought "firm" cars for hundreds less! As in all types of negotiating, you never know until you ask.

Throughout the three phases of bargaining, whenever the seller comes back with a new offer, make some immediate gesture indicating that it's unacceptable. Grunt, moan, raise your eyebrows, flinch, scream, do something to show that the offer they just made is still out of the ball park. If you don't show some sign of dismay, the seller will think the offer he just made is within reason, since you didn't seem bothered by it.

When making your first offer, always give yourself bargaining room to come up to your target purchase price. If the asking price is $4,500 and you only want to pay $4,000, then offer $3,500. If you offer $4,000, the seller will counter-offer, expecting you to come up in price to meet him. In this case, it would probably be at $4,250, which is $250 more than you wanted to pay.

Why not offer the $4,000 as a take- it-or-leave-it offer? Because, first of all, if the person you're dealing with is any kind of a negotiator, he will expect you to come up a little more in price regardless of you saying take it or leave it. Second, if the person you're dealing with isn't too hip on negotiating, he may let it go for even lower than $4,000.

Another important tip in negotiating is assuming what the seller's target price is. When you don't see the word "firm" in the ad, always count on the seller padding the price to allow some negotiating room. Although it's no guarantee, most cars advertised at $2,200, $2,300, $2,400, or $2,500 will likely have a $2,000 seller's target price, while cars listed at $3,200, $3,300, $3,400, and $3,500 will likely have a $3,000 seller's target price, so on and so forth. As a general rule of thumb, always count on $200 to $500 added to a seller's target price. When reading the ads, you can use this information to stay within your budget.

And one last note. You can apply these negotiation techniques when you go to purchase a house or a business and save yourself thousands. Should you need some work done to your property and a contractor presents you with a bid, that bid is also open to negotiation. Should you ever find yourself as a purchaser in a corporate environment, shrewd negotiating can save the company hundreds of thousands and earn promotions. So learning this art by practicing on used cars can certainly lead to much bigger savings later in life.

TRANSFER OF VEHICLE OWNERSHIP

Because all states vary, you will need to contact your motor vehicle department ahead of time to find out exactly what is required when a change of ownership occurs. Currently in California, you need a signed Certificate of Title, also known as a pink slip, a Release of Liability sent in by the seller, a Smog Certificate, and an Odometer Disclosure Statement.

Before you hand over any cash, the seller should have in possession a Certificate of Title which proves he is the owner of the vehicle that he is selling. On the title should be the Vehicle Identification Number (VIN), license plate number, year, make, and model of the car. The VIN should match that on the car. Check these numbers BEFORE you buy the car, not after.

Starting with all 1969 models, you will find the VIN on the dash under the windshield on the driver's side, which is read from outside through the glass. Most newer autos will also have the VIN stamped on a plate that is mounted on the firewall under the hood. On some sports cars and imports you may find the VIN on the driver's side door jam as well. Prior to 1969, the placement of the VIN was random. Look for a stamped plate around the engine compartment area or in the door jams.

If you can't find a stamped plate with the VIN anywhere, if there seems to be some tampering, or if the seller has lost the title to their car, quietly leave. I recommend that you call your state police department with the car's license plate number in hand. Ask them to check it out for you. You wouldn't want to buy a stolen car, would you?

The seller's signature on the title releases his interest. If there is a lienholder on the title, such as a bank, then the lienholder needs to sign to release his interest as well. Do not hand over any cash until the lienholder has signed; otherwise, you will be assuming what is still owed on the car.

In California, the seller should have you fill out a Release of Liability. This protects him in case you should have an accident or receive a parking ticket before you get the chance to register the car in your name. It is the seller's responsibility to have this filled out and sent in, not the buyer's.

Starting with all 1966 models registered in California, a smog certificate is required every time a vehicle changes hands. According to the DMV (Department of Motor Vehicles), it should be taken care of by the seller; however, the seller can negotiate this with the buyer, making it the buyer's responsibility. If this is the case, get the seller to compensate you for the cost in the sales price.

So, Californians, when shopping around for your mechanic it is important to find one who does smog inspections, or at least knows what to look for in the area of smog equipment. You don't want to end up with a car that has smog equipment missing. It could cost you a bundle to replace. YOU WON'T BE ALLOWED TO REGISTER THE VEHICLE UNTIL IT PASSES SMOG!

The Odometer Disclosure Statement is a new form required by the DMV only for vehicles with the old style of title. Since you won't know in advance which title the seller will have, pick up a form at your nearby DMV and have the seller fill this out reqardless. It's a simple form to complete where the seller confirms whether the mileage on the odometer is actual or not. Should a seller lie about this, he could get a big fat fine and possibly a jail term to boot.

Another requirement in California is a Bill of Sale when the seller's name isn't the same name as that on the title. It is a good policy, however, to make out a bill of sale for your own records, regardless. If you don't have an official Bill of Sale form, you can easily hand-write one. Just make sure you put down the year, make, model, VIN, and plate number along with your name, the seller's name, and the agreed-upon price. You don't need anything fancy, just a sentence or two describing how you are buying such-and-such vehicle from so-and-so for X number of dollars on this date, etc. Make sure the seller signs and dates it.

Although the current registration certificate isn't required for transfer of ownership in California, you want to be aware of vehicles with out-dated registrations. Unless a current non-operational status has been filed with the state, a car with an out-dated registration translates to stiff penalties for the next victim who registers it. These could amount to hundreds of dollars. So if you're looking at a car that hasn't been registered in a few years, you better find out from your motor vehicle department how much is owed in back registration penalties before you purchase or you could get stung.

SALVAGE TITLES

A salvage title can mean several things, all of which are bad. The car may have been stolen, stripped, and recovered; it could have been in a major accident; or worse yet, it could have been damaged in a flood. In any case, when the insurance company finds the car is not worth repairing, the a car receives a salvage title from the DMV before getting auctioned off to a junk dealer, repair shop, or body man who will make the repairs with the intention of selling the patched-up car for a profit.

The "Salvage" stamp on the title remains there for the life of the car. To no surprise, the car sells for much less than cars with a clean title. To be on the safe side, any car with a salvage title should get an automatic failure from you.

THE SEVEN GOLDEN RULES OF NEGOTIATION

1) Control your emotions - no gloating when you find a car you adore
2) Precondition, precondition, precondition
3) Negotiate to the lowest possible price before going to your mechanic
4) Negotiate to the lowest possible price after the car has been inspected
5) If negotiation doesn't go your way, always remain polite and professional
6) Check over the title and registration documents thoroughly
7) Don't buy a salvage title car
8) Never be in a hurry to buy a used car

PART II:

HOW TO BUY A USED CAR
FROM A DEALER

♪ ♫ ♪
HELLO   FRIEND.....HAVE I GOT A DEAL FOR YOU !

CHAPTER 6:

DEALING WITH DEALERS

Those of you who are buying a used car through a private party have my permission to skip this section and fast forward to Chapter 8: **Selling Your Used Car**. Those of you who are taking the dealership route, proceed carefully.

So far I have only talked about buying a used car from a private party, mainly because it's the best way to go. From a private party you pay less and get more, rather than paying more and getting less, which is usually the case with a dealer. But if you are in a situation where you need to buy a car as soon as possible, or have been patiently looking for a long time and the small town you live in offers little action in the private-party used car market, you'll be forced to deal with a dealer. Just remember, out on the used car lot it's a dog-eat-dog world and you're wearing milk bone shorts!

Before you step onto any used car lot you must prepare yourself for high pressure sales tactics, con games, double-talk, and phony add-ons. Knowledge and preparation is your best defense against dealership shenanigans and it's your only real hope in avoiding a trip to the cleaners.

If you studied my book this far, you should know what model(s) are for you, how to select a mechanic, how to inspect and test drive a car, and how to negotiate with the seller. What I will cover in this chapter is how to select a dealer, salesman tactics, buyer tactics, and dealer finance and warranty information.

THE WAY DEALERS WORK

In dealing with a dealer, it helps to understand the way most dealerships work. As a whole, the dealership's main objective is to buy your trade-in for as little as possible while selling you their car, and extras, for as much as possible. The means of accomplishing this is through a simple hierarchy of staff.

Starting from the top, there's the sales manager who will oversee and give the okay to each sale. Next are the closers or finance managers. Their job is to make you forget about all those promises the salesman made, sell you some extras, and finalize the deal. Then there are the salesmen themselves. On most dealership lots they are the ones outside greeting the consumer, going on test drives, finding out if you're a "today" buyer and, if you're not, promising whatever it takes to lure you into the sales office and turn you into a "today" buyer.

Should you get lured into the salesman's office, all those carrots he dangled out on the lot will be neatly eliminated one by one. If you are easy, the salesman will usually work on you right up until the contract and paperwork needs signing. Then the closer comes in and tries to sell you some last-minute extras as he gradually goes over the paper work.

If you turn out to be a tough customer, the salesman will hand you over to another salesman, manager, or closer early in the game. The next person will come in with a fresh set of negotiation tactics and will want to start from scratch, ignoring any ground you gained with the first salesman. It's a great way to wear you down. There's a whole army of salesmen, but there's only one of you.

That, in a nutshell, is the dealership story. Some of the smaller ones may combine the salesman's and closer's duties, but they always have a sales manager (boss) to clear things with.

A WORD ON FINANCING

MAKE SURE YOU HAVE IT IN ORDER BEFORE YOU ENTER A USED CAR LOT! You could start by checking with your own bank, but it would be wise to shop around by phone to find out who offers the lowest Annual Percentage Rate (APR) on auto loans.

After finding the best rate and getting pre-approved, you will know how much the loan will cost you, the amount of the monthly payments, the length of the term, and hence, how much car you can afford.

Hopefully you have decent credit and this won't be a problem. If you have bad credit, some dealers can get you financed but you will be at their mercy and pay dearly. They will be happy to set you up with a loan where you pay interest on interest or pay off all the interest in the first year of the loan. This may be good for them, but it is a bum deal for the consumer. Stay away from these types of loans and stick with a simple interest loan with a competitive APR, preferably without a prepayment penalty (in case you win the lottery).

Having outside financing also allows you the option for a powerful negotiation tactic that will be illustrated later in this chapter. So get your financing in order.

TO BE OR NOT TO BE ALONE

When you go used car shopping, there are advantages and disadvantages to going by yourself or with a friend. One advantage of going alone is that dealers love to play off your kid's or your spouse's emotions and are excellent at reading looks that you and your spouse will be exchanging. Remember when I mentioned about playing deadpan? You see a car that really excites you but you act as if you could care less. This is much easier to do alone and will work wonders when it's time to negotiate.

Going alone also gives you a powerful excuse to walk away from a deal that isn't going your way. Whether you're married or single you say, "I need to go home and talk it over with my spouse," or "I need to bring my spouse by tomorrow. After all, it will be his/her car." When the dealer insists on driving the car over to your house for your spouse's approval, you respond with, "My spouse is at work" or "My spouse is out of town," etc.

However, bringing a friend along has its advantages also. When shopping for cars you have two things to deal with at the same time: talkative salesmen and your inspection. By bringing a friend, you have the advantage of letting your partner occupy the babbling salesman while you concentrate on your inspection.

Your friend or spouse can also work wonders at the negotiation table for confirming offers, value of your trade-in, etc. Instead of one person to sway, the salesman has two.

So which do you do? If you are a partnership, that is, married, go together and stick together during negotiation. And leave the kids home. But if you're a strong-headed single person, go alone. You can deal with it. However, if you are single and easily influenced by others, you're going to get into trouble if you go alone. Bring a friend and tell him or her up front exactly what you are looking for and how much you can afford. That way he or she can keep you in check if a salesman starts talking you into something you didn't initially want or can't afford.

CHOOSING A DEALER

I strongly recommend staying away from the small-time non-dealership lots. You know the kind. They have names like Crazy Joe's Used Cars and have a small mobile office parked on their lot. Don't even bother. Stick with the reputable, new-car dealerships like Chevrolet, Ford, Toyota, etc. They all have used car lots because of the trade-ins they continuously accept.

If you have heard good word of mouth about any of these new dealerships, make them your first stop in your hunt for a decent used car. If you haven't heard a word from anyone about which dealers are respectable, start asking around. Neighbors, co-workers, friends, and relatives would be good places to start.

The reason you should stick with the new-car dealerships is because the cars they accept as trade-ins are likely to be from private owners rather than from car rental fleets or bank repos like the small lots frequently peddle. New-car dealerships will also have a better warranty program and the facilities to provide service. They are more likely to stand behind their warranty to uphold their good name.

This is what you want to pay particular attention to when asking your friends' experiences with their dealers. How did they handle you when you brought the car in for repairs covered under warranty? Did they take care of you right away and fix the problem the first time, or did they give you the run-around, hoping you would just go away?

One more thing about new-car dealerships. If they accept a clunker for a trade-in, rather than sell it from their lot and take a chance on someone getting a lemon, they will wholesale it out to an auto broker who will, in turn, auction it to a non-dealership lot like Crazy Joe's, which is another good reason to stay away from them. If I can sway you into only dealing with new-car dealerships--and hopefully by now I have--then your chances of getting a dependable used auto just doubled.

BEFORE GOING TO THE LOTS

A big time saver before you go to the dealerships is to call in advance and ask for the used car department. When they connect you, ask for the used car sales manager and find out if it's okay to have their used cars checked out by your mechanic--provided they have something you're interested in, of course.

Remember, you only want YOUR mechanic to check the car out and not the dealership's mechanic as some may insist. And make sure it's okay with them to take their car to your mechanic. Some may only allow your mechanic to come inspect it at their lot. This is too much to expect from your busy mechanic, so don't ask him.

Most dealerships will allow you take the car in. But if they don't, it's better to find out over the phone rather than after you've spent time inspecting and test driving. If the sales manager says that all the cars have already been checked over and are covered under warranty, tell him you're sorry you couldn't do business and scratch him off your list.

If they do allow you to take the car to your mechanic, this would be a good opportunity to ask if they have any of the particular model(s) that you're looking for. If they do, find out what year and how much it's selling for. Also, make sure you get the person's name for reference later.

Keep in mind that many salesmen will lie and tell you they have just what you're looking for at an incredibly low price. When you hightail it down there, the salesman tells you, "You're too late. We just sold it. But over here I have a real nice such and such..." and of course, it's for much more money than what they quoted you over the phone. This is the common bait-and-switch trick.

The best way to thwart this is to ask more specific questions about the car like, "Is it standard or automatic?" "Does it have air or any other power features?" "How many miles are on it?" "What color is it?" Judging the way they answer should be enough to tip you off to their honesty.

With your list of dealerships in hand, you need to make one more call. Contact your local Better Business Bureau and ask if there have been any complaints filed against the dealerships you plan to visit. If there were, find out how each complaint was addressed by the dealer. Judging by the Bureau's response, you may want to delete those respective dealers from your list.

WHAT TO EXPECT AT THE LOTS

If you find yourself at a car lot and you don't see any of the models you desire, it's worth it to ask the salesman if there are any that will be available soon. They may just have one that's getting detailed that will be on the lot tomorrow. However, if he doesn't know of any, thank him and you're off to the next new car dealership lot--no ifs, ands, or buts.

When a salesman discovers he doesn't have the model(s) you want he will immediately try to talk you into a "similar" model. Of course "similar" in a dealer's mind may mean four doors and four tires. Or, a dealer may ask why you have decided on that particular model(s). Regardless of your response he may try scare tactics and describe how his "friend" had one of those same models and it was a lemon. He may even be bold enough to say how his dealership refuses to accept those cars as trade-ins because of how bad they are, which is exactly why they don't have any. If you've done your research, don't buy it for a minute. Most likely the real facts are that the dealer's "friend" is imaginary and the only reason they don't have any of those particular models is because they're such hot sellers.

When dealing with dealers you have to think like a dealer. They look at you as a potential sale especially if you appear to be a "today" buyer. They know if they let you walk off the lot to "shop around," chances are they'll never see you again. This is exactly why most salesmen pull out all the stops to sell you a car today. So, if they don't have the exact model(s) you're looking for, get out of there quick!

GETTING FOCUSED

When you do come across the model(s) that you are looking for, price will be your main concern. Find out what the car is selling for before you spend your time looking it over. If there isn't a price marked on the car, you will need to ask a salesman. Many dealerships do this deliberately so you are forced to find a salesman. If the price of the car is above what you can afford, remember: all car prices, whether new or used, are marked up to give the salesmen negotiating room. How much they are marked up depends on a lot of factors.

With a window sticker price of $7,995 on a used car, it may be possible to get it for $7,000, or even less, but there's no way you'll get a thousand bucks knocked off a car selling for $2,495. So, as a general rule of thumb figure on getting a car for 10% to 15% less than the sticker price. This means $1,000 to $1,500 less on a $10,000 car and $500 to $750 less on a car selling for $5,000. I would like to say right now that negotiating this much off the price is no easy feat. Salesmen are shrewd negotiators. They do this every day. So no matter how many books you read, they will still have an edge on you.

However, I want you to adopt a slight variation of the "rules were made to be broken" saying, which is, *"salesmen were made to be broken."* You can break them. There's nothing keeping you from getting up and walking out the door when the negotiating isn't going anywhere. The fact that there are plenty of other dealerships around gives you a lot of power. Always tell yourself, I don't have to have this car. There are plenty of other dealerships and plenty of other cars.

When you find something in your price range, start your inspection just as I have outlined back in the **Checking the Beast** chapter. Like it or not, a pesky salesman will find you (if one hasn't already) and start to ask prequalifying questions to see if you are a "today" buyer. Somewhere in there he will ask questions about you or your family and strike a nerve with you. You will warm up to him, if he's good.

Salesmen like to run the show and they do so by asking question after question. You needn't answer every question they ask, and ignoring them is a good way to put the message across that you're tired of their questioning. For persistent salesmen, the best way to turn it around is by answering a question with a question.

A babbling salesman hovering over you and trying to rush you during your visual inspection can be very distracting. Take your time and keep referring to your inspection checklist from Appendix B so that you don't overlook anything.

A good tip during your inspection is to make sure you touch every scratch, ding, and flaw on the car in front of the salesman. Is there a crack in the dash or a tear in the seat? Run your fingers over it. Is there oil grime on the engine? Stick your finger in it. You needn't say anything when you do this. Just make sure the salesman sees you do this so he knows you know it's there. By the way, this is exactly what the salesman will do when he looks over your trade-in. It's a great preconditioning psychology designed to soften a would-be tight negotiator. Believe me, it works.

Of course, while all this is going on the salesman will be babbling on about this or that, trying to distract you and pretending he doesn't notice what you're doing, but don't worry, he does. If the car hasn't automatically failed for damaged frame, rust, etc., tell the salesman you wish to take it for a test drive.

Most salesmen will have a route that they take everyone on. This is okay as long as it offers freeway speeds and a quiet street to check the brakes and reverse, so request this up front. Go through the test drive just as I outlined in the **Test Drive** chapter, making notes on your checklist of anything out of the ordinary. If everything seems to be okay, tell the salesman you wish to take it to your mechanic for his inspection. The salesman may object, but because you already cleared it with the sales manager over the phone (remember his/her name), the salesman can't say no.

It's worth it to ask the salesman about the previous owners. He may know about them, he may not. Just don't fall for the "this car was owned by a little old lady who only drove it to church and the market on Sundays" line. It's the oldest one in the book. If he does know who the owners were, ask for the phone number so you can call later and talk to them about their car. At this point in the game the previous owners would have no reason to lie about any problems that may be hidden.

Set up an appointment as soon as possible with your mechanic and have the salesman meet you there with the car. Or the dealer may ask that you sign a borrowed car contract and let you take it over yourself. Just make sure before you sign that there are no numbers involved. You are not agreeing to buy this car for a specified amount of money if it checks out okay. If you decide that you are interested you will negotiate a price later.

Never leave a deposit for taking a car to your mechanic. Some dealers may try to pull this. If the car doesn't check out the salesman will use your deposit as bait to lure you to another car. If a dealer requires that you leave a deposit and/or sign a contract that involves a price, walk away. There are plenty of other dealers who will accommodate you.

Don't forget to provide your mechanic with the checklist from your inspection of anything that was in question. When he's finished the mechanic should meet with you privately without the salesman around. Right away your mechanic will tell you whether the car's worth pursuing or not. If it is worth pursuing, you can use whatever solid information came from the mechanic's report as bargaining leverage which, by the way, carries a lot of weight at the negotiation table.

THE GAMES DEALERS PLAY

Negotiating with a used car salesman is going to be a lot different from negotiating with a private party. As a matter of fact, haggling with a private party is a cake walk compared to a used car salesman. You earn every dollar you talk a salesman down. It's certainly not for the weak-hearted. If you are, the salesman will have his way with you.

Plan on spending anywhere from two to three hours for negotiating and the paperwork involved in closing the deal. Salesmen have all kinds of tricks when it comes to negotiating. Here are the most common ploys and the best way to deal with them.

Urgency and The Other Customer

Considering that you are after cars with great reliability records, you will probably find many salesmen trying the urgency tactic on you. They may very well be selling the model you want like hot cakes, but they like to exaggerate and talk it up good. "I have three other parties interested in this car. If you don't take it right now, it'll be gone by the end of the day." Suddenly you are backed into a corner.

Or it may happen this way: you are in the middle of stalemate negotiations when the phone rings, and you hear the salesman say something like, "Oh hello mister so-and- so. No, I still have the sedan, but I'm negotiating with someone right now. I'd be happy to call you back if the deal falls through."

Don't fall for the urgency ploy. The three other customers may have been from the past two weeks or may not exist at all. As for the phone call during negotiations, it's probably a buddy co-worker calling from the next office. The way to nullify the saleman's urgency tactic is by displaying an "oh well" cavalier attitude and mention that there are plenty of other cars available at other dealerships. YOU DON'T HAVE TO HAVE THIS CAR. Keep thinking like this and you'll do okay.

If I Could...

A favorite sales tactic for the salesman is getting you to commit early in the negotiations: the "If I could... would you buy today?" routine. "If I could get $2,000 for your trade-in, would you take our car today?" or "If I could get the price down another $200, would you buy today?" When you say yes to questions like these you are commiting yourself. And that's a commitment they will hold you to. Meanwhile the salesman promises nothing. He is only saying *if* I could. That's no promise. To avoid getting trapped into a commitment tell him that if he comes through you will continue negotiations and work with him to close the deal.

Low Monthly Payments

Another favorite negotiation tactic combines the 'If I could...' with the amount of your monthly payments. They won't talk car price at all. Instead, they place you into a comfortable monthly payment plan. "Would you take the car if I could get the payments down to $200 a month?" "Would you take the car if I could get the payments down to $180 a month?" They keep going down until you say "Okay! I can afford that." Meanwhile your down payment has gone way up and the term of your loan has been stretched, but they don't mention this, of course. Instead, they hook you with those tempting low monthly payments.

This is not the way to negotiate a car deal. You will come out a loser every time. To keep this from happening, tell the salesman right out that if he is to sell you a car today, then he must negotiate on the total price of the car which, by the way, is to be negotiated separately from the total price you receive for your trade-in.

Delay of Game

Salesmen are good at wearing people down. One way they do this is by making you wait forever to receive an offer on your trade-in from their manager. Or several times during negotiations they will go ask their sales manager if they can accept a lower offer. When they leave they are gone for a good 15-20 minutes while you sit wondering what could possibly be taking so long. Meanwhile, your salesman is in the breakroom B.S.'ing with other co-workers who are playing the same game. They will keep doing this, waiting for you to break down, lose your patience and give in to their price. They wouldn't do it if didn't work, but now you know better.

Let's say your salesman's name is John. The first time John says he has to go clear something with his manager grab him before he goes out the door and consult your watch and say "Okay, John, I have 7:25 on my watch. I'll give you five minutes. If you're not back here by 7:30 I'm heading out the door." And stick to what you say. He may try to call your bluff. If he's not back in five minutes, get up and slowly walk to your car. Trust me, he will come running after you. There's no way he'll take a chance on losing a potential sale. Do this every time he goes to his sales manager and you will nullify his delay of game.

Salesman Turnover

When a salesman has a tough buyer on his hands and isn't getting anywhere, he will excuse himself to his manager and then either his manager or another salesman will step in to try and negotiate with you. There's only one of you, but there's a whole army of salesmen on staff. The theory is that after dickering back and forth with the first salesman for 45 minutes you are likely to break down when a fresh salesman comes in and starts working you with his best haggling verbiage. They wouldn't do if it didn't work.

The best way to handle salesman turnover is by holding firm to what you have negotiated for. The new salesman will try to revoke your efforts in one smooth swoop, but you won't let him. If the salesman seems to ignore you, get up and start to walk out and see how fast the salesman stops his game. Remember, you don't have to have this car and your shoes aren't glued to the floor. Don't be afraid to walk.

Similar to salesman turnover is when two or more salesmen gang up on you. If this occurs, refuse to negotiate. Tell them you're sorry but you only negotiate with one person at a time. If they ignore you, head for your car and watch how fast they grant your request.

Misplaced Keys

When you want to trade in your car you should have your title and registration with you to show that you are a serious buyer. Salesmen like to get your keys and documents in their possession. Should the negotiations get tough and you decide to walk, you're stuck until they produce your keys and/or papers, which have suddenly been misplaced. Of course, while their manager is hunting them down the salesman has bought more time to pressure you into a deal you don't want.

The way to thwart this tactic and create an edge for yourself at the same time is to have the documents on you but tell the salesman they are in the glove box. Then give him a spare set of keys to allow his manager to check and test drive your car. Later, when they ask the whereabouts of your documents, act absent-minded and suddenly remember they are in your purse/pocket but do not relinquish them. Tell them you had the papers out earlier when you were visiting the dealership down the street.

This creates an edge for you because now, in the dealer's eyes, you have been out shopping around and you are looking to see who's going to offer the best deal. They know now that if they are to make a sale with you they will have to bend more than usual. It also gives you credibility later, during negotiations, when you tell them you saw a better deal down the street.

The Guilt Trip

Another tactic salesmen use is the guilt trip. They always have family pictures prominately displayed on their desk. Then they bring up their kids and the braces they will soon be needing, etc. Pack your bags because they're about to take you on a guilt trip. They will make you feel guilty for wanting to talk them down in price, especially when it's their profit they are losing. Don't get suckered by this. You have your problems too. I've known salesmen who use this ploy who don't even have kids. Besides, even if they do have kids who need braces, they can easily afford it. Used car salesmen make more money than you want to know.

Stupidity

You are stupid. The salesman talks circles around you and makes the assumption that anyone who can't understand what he is saying is stupid. You have no idea what he's talking about, yet you are afraid to ask because in his eyes you'll be stupid. It's a great way to get you to proceed into something that you don't understand. Not good. Don't let them do this to you. If there is something that doesn't make sense, stop them and ask them to back up and explain. Make them reword what they are saying. It's the ones who don't question the salesmen who are stupid.

Yes Deposit, No Return

You may come across a salesman who requests a deposit in order to continue negotiations. His claim is that it shows you are serious. Never, ever give a deposit until an agreement in price has been reached and finalized on paper. If you do give them a deposit up front, they will use it get you to succumb to their price. If you don't give in, they keep your deposit. Though they can't legally do this they can still have a lot of fun in the process.

    If you fall prey to this, threaten to notify the Better Business Bureau and the Federal Trade Commission. If this doesn't get your deposit back, hopefully your deposit was in the form of a check and you can put a stop payment on it as soon as possible.

The Trip to Aruba

One of my personal favorites is where the salesman informs you about a contest the dealership is having in which the salesman with the highest sales wins a trip to Hawaii, St. Thomas, or whatever exotic location the salesman happens to pick for the day. Of course, your salesman is only one sale short of winning the trip, or is neck-and-neck with another salesman and needs your sale desperately.

Don't get suckered by this. Even if it were true, why should you help out the salesman by paying more than you should for a car? You work hard for your money too. No one is sending you to Aruba.

BUYER TACTICS

List of Rules

Before any negotiations start, mention to the salesman how the last time you bought a car you had a bad experience with the sales staff (at another dealership, of course). You tell him that if you are to buy a car from them they must read and sign to your list of negotiation rules. You then hand him a copy of your neatly typed list designed to strip him of his powers:

>   **Rule #1:** Our negotiations are to be dealt with in three separate steps. First, the price on our trade-in is reached. Second, the price on your car is decided. And, lastly, the financing is figured out. No negotiating through monthly payments allowed.
>   **Rule #2:** No confusing or misleading terminology or numbers allowed. Anything not understood will be reworded until the buyer fully understands what is being presented.
>   **Rule #3:** We will deal with only one salesman at a time. No double-teaming.
>   **Rule #4:** Any additional concessions (extras) will be in writing on the contract.
>   **Rule #5:** Respect. We respect you as a dealer who needs to make a profit in order to survive. You respect us as customers whom you need as a means for survival. No disrespectful comments allowed from either side.
>   **Rule # 6:** Any violation of the above rules will stop the negotiation process immediately, and the buyer shall not continue until all rules are adhered to.

Most salesmen will object to signing to these rules because they know they're signing away most of their negotiation edge. You need to act sincere when you present them with this and describe the terrible experience you had. Finish by telling them if they don't want to agree to your rules that's fine, you will go somewhere else to buy a car. They most likely will sign. Once they sign, keep a copy in front of you for reference, and if they should break one of the rules, call them on it. You can't proceed until they follow the rules!

Your Trade-in

With no intention of trading in your car, tell the salesman before negotiations that you wish to trade in your current car as part of the down payment because you don't want the hassle of selling it. When the salesman offers you his first ridiculously low offer, object and get him to come up a little more. When he increases his offer a little, object again, but then give in.

Later, when you continue negotiations, the salesman will be more flexible and willing to come down on his price knowing that he will make a killing on your trade-in. After grinding him down as low as you can and agreeing on a price, have him draw up a contract with the figures. Then, just before you are about to sign, you have a sudden change of heart and decide you'd rather not trade in your car after all. When the salesman's face falls, look at him and say, "I'm sorry. I forgot about my nephew who needs a car. What's the big deal anyway? The car isn't worth anything, just like you said."

In order to get away with this you have to have some backup for a down payment, so you better have a couple of grand in your checking account. You also want to object on the dealer's first low-ball offer for your trade-in because if you give in too easily the salesman may catch on to you and play hard ball with you all the way through. You want to object and then play dumb like you don't care about your old car and would just as soon get rid of it.

Your Financing

With no intention of financing through the dealer, and having already made arrangements with an outside lender that offers excellent rates, tell the dealer that you need a loan and want them to take care of all the financing. When you fill out the loan application, give them the impression that you hate to deal with banks and figures, etc.

If you did not present the **List of Rules** tactic, the salesman will try talking to you in terms of monthly payments, but you need to switch him back to total price of the car in order to chew him down. Tell him you're not worried about the amount of monthly payments because you don't have an affordability problem. Tell him you wish to settle on the full price of the car first and then you'll adjust the payments to your liking via length of term.

Because the dealership is arranging the financing, and making extra money from it, they will be a little more flexible in lowering the price of the car. After grinding them down as far as you can, and after they draw up a contract, you check the figures and then suddenly have a change of mind. You decide that you are going to finance through an outside company because you just remembered one that offers great rates--unless, of course, the dealer can beat them.

When the salesman scoffs at you, insist that you can have the money in a couple of days. Most dealers' policies allow one week to come up with the money from an outside source. If they need it sooner, you can get it the next day because you have already been guaranteed a loan. Leave the dealership with the mention that if you can't qualify for the outside loan you will finance through them. Of course, you need some money for a down payment before they let you drive your new car home.

Even if the dealer doesn't let you fly with this, you can accept their high-interest loan and, when the first payment comes due, pay it off in full with your low-interest loan. Before you do this, though, you want to make sure that there aren't any stiff prepayment penalties in the dealer's loan or a steep loan processing fee from your bank that would negate the difference you would save in the lower interest loan. Depending on the penalties and loan fees, a difference of one or two interest points can be borderline. Figure this out in advance.

Buyer's Delay of Game
Similar to the salesman's delay of game tactic is the buyer wearing down the sales staff. After finding a car you like and having your mechanic check it over earlier in the day, show up about 60 to 90 minutes before a dealer closes. You have just finished a light dinner, had some coffee, are refreshed and just want to take your time in purchasing a car tonight.

The sales staff, however, have been working all day, are tired, and ready to go home. By the time you test drive the car again, fill out a loan app, and allow the sales manager to check out your trade-in, you will have reached closing time with still another hour or two of negotiations ahead. Because you are a "today" buyer, the salesman certainly won't kick you out but he will want to speed up negotiations and close the deal. Most of the time the salesmen are more flexible in price and willing to deal just for the sake of going home.

Buyer's Urgency

Much in the same way the salesman tries to instill the urgency "buy before it's gone," you can create a similar kind of urgency to lay upon the salesman himself. It's called the "lower your price now or I buy somewhere else" urgency. You must lay it on the line with force like the whole deal hinges on the salesman's decision to reduce the price. If your pitch doesn't come out strong and he calls your bluff, get up and start walking.

Respect

When you are negotiating with the sales manager and he claims he is at his bottom, this would be a good time to stroke him with your respect speech. A good respect speech would go something like this:

"Mr. Sales Manager, I have a lot of respect for you and your dealership. My wife and I have heard many good things from our friends who have made purchases here, and the excellent treatment by your staff so far confirms those claims. Now, I understand that you must make a profit on each deal and there's nothing wrong with you making a profit. I don't have a problem with that. We all have bills to pay. However, if we are to come to terms today then we have to agree on what would be a fair deal for both of us. I am ready to buy this car today, but only if it's a fair deal. Now, I'm willing to offer you $___ for this car and I know it isn't a huge profit for you, but nonetheless it is a profit. Otherwise, if I don't buy from you today then I buy from someone else tomorrow. So what do you say? Do we have a deal?"

He probably won't accept your offer, but if you come across sincerely he will likely lower his price significantly. If you botch up your speech you will fall flat on your face and gain nothing. Don't use the respect speech if you aren't a good actor.

Forfeit Dealer's Warranty

If something should happen and *if* the dealer doesn't claim owner abuse and *if* the dealership honors its warranty and *if* the term hasn't elasped and *if* the warranty covers the problem, the buyer will likely share some of the repair cost anyway. This is too many *ifs* for something that is unlikely to go wrong with a car that was inspected by a mechanic who you trust and who gave it a clean bill of auto health.

You should consider passing on the dealer's warranty in lieu of a significant reduction in the sales price. Save this tactic for the end of negotiations when you announce the amount of the reduction hinges upon the sale of the car.

Sleep On It
Another last-ditch effort to get the salesman to lower his price one more time is by telling him you wish to sleep on it. Use this ploy only when you are at the end of your negotiations and ready to either buy or pass. Mention how you would have wanted to take the car tonight, but at his price you're going to have to sleep on it. Stand up, shake the salesman's hand, and tell him how unfortunate it is that you couldn't meet in price...and watch him start adjusting his figures.

DEALER ADD-ONS

In California, the only fees a dealer must charge on top of the selling price (which should include all extra options like air-conditioning, floor mats, etc.), would be state sales tax, registration fees, and a $10 transfer fee. The state also allows the maximum of $35 each for smog and documentary fees. Nothing more. If you reside in another state, contact you local motor vehicle department about what your state requires.

All those other official-sounding charges are nothing more than a ploy to get more money out of you, so refuse to pay them. They may come in the form of a Delivery and Handling Fee or D&H Fee. Then there's the Vehicle Handling Fee or VHF Fee. And let's not forget the Maintenance Fee or Prep Fee and the many other creative charges.

Any one or all of these fees could be tagged onto your bill ranging from $25 to hundreds of dollars. Most people accept them when the dealer informs them that they charge everyone these fees, but now you know better. Refuse to pay them and threaten to walk out if they don't remove them. Believe me, they will drop them and you will have saved even more money.

Other dealer add-ons come in the form of extras they try to sell you to go along with your car. Rustproofing is a common one, but it does little good to cover over the rust that's already started on a four-year-old used car. Pass on the rustproofing. Besides, today's cars are more rust resistant than those of the '70s.

Another dealer add-on is an extended warranty or service contract. These may seem tempting because you're buying a used car with a few miles on it and something is bound to go wrong. The price of the warranty could easily be absorbed into your loan for only a few more dollars a month.

Forget the extended warranty. You already bought one when you paid your mechanic to find out if there were any hidden problems with the car, so why pay hundreds of dollars for something that might go wrong during the short term of the warranty?

In addition, the dealer may try to weasel out of repairs and claim owner abuse if you don't have every receipt for every oil change and maintenance service required by the manufacturer. In addition, most of these service contracts have deductibles, same as an insurance policy, only this is an insurance policy that you don't need.

Other extras they may try to sell you are paint preserver to restore the luster to your car or fabric treatment for your upholstery. Forget those too. You can buy a can of polishing compound and fabric protector from your auto supply store and do it yourself if it needs it. The difference is, you'll save plenty of money.

THE TRADING GAME

Most dealerships accept good trade-ins on their used cars, and for the buyer it's like killing two birds with one stone. You buy a new car and sell off your old car in one sitting. The convenience is tempting but you pay dearly for that convenience. My advice here is to sell the car yourself. The dealer will offer you a price way below what your car is worth and will also hold a negotiating edge.

Let's say the current market value of your well-maintained car is $3,200. The dealer may offer you $1,000 if he's feeling generous. The car you want from the dealer is listed at $5,995 which means you can now get it for $4,995. Already you're getting excited, but wait until you try any further negotiations. The dealer holds the negotiating edge because he already came down $1,000 in price. He will claim he couldn't possibly come down any more without losing money. He makes it sound as if he is going to take your trade-in and throw it away when, in fact, the dealer will be making double profits in one deal.

However, if you decided to sell the car on your own you could easily get $2,500 for it, probably in a week or two, or even more $ if you didn't mind taking your time. Now the price of $5,995 will be offset by $2,500 instead of a measly $1,000. Clearly, selling your own car is the way to go.

WARRANTIES

Most reputable dealers will offer some sort of warranty on their used vehicles. In many cases, to keep the warranty valid, they require you to bring the car back for maintenance service at the dealership from which you bought it. There they may charge pricey fees for oil changes, etc., which can get costly and time consuming. And for those who prefer to do their own oil changes, they may cancel out their warranty without realizing it.

Keep in mind, a warranty is only as good as the dealer who writes it. If the dealer doesn't require that you bring the car in for maintenance and something breaks down, he immediately points a finger at you, claiming car abuse. You didn't do the required maintenance. Dealers are notorious for weaseling out of their warranties. If the car received a good report from your mechanic, I strongly recommend passing on the dealer's warranty (as previously mentioned) in exchange for a significant price reduction.

For your reference, however, here is some warranty information you may find valuable in helping you to make a decision.

Factory Warranty
The warranty that comes with every new car is a factory warranty and is usually transferrable to the second owner if it hasn't expired. Those of you in the market for a one-or two-year-old car, keep this in mind. Your dealer may get a sudden case of amnesia and fail to mention this to you with the hope of selling you a service contract on which he can make a commission. To find out for sure if the car has a transferable warranty, call the manufacturer's zone office in your area. They will need the Vehicle Identification Number of the car in question.

As Is - No Warranty
As mentioned before, the buyer assumes all costs for any future repairs. Avoid cars on the dealer's lot marked with an 'as is' warranty. To me this is an indication that the dealer knows of a problem and won't back it with a warranty for a reason. And that's a reason you don't need to find out.

Full Warranty

A full warranty is when the dealer agrees to make repairs without any charge for parts and labor. The warranty is for a specified amount of time and/or miles and will only cover those components stated in the contract.

Limited Warranty

Basically the same as a full warranty except the buyer shares a certain percentage of the repair costs.

Extended Warranty

Usually referred to as a service contract, an extended warranty is always offered on new cars and most used cars that don't have high mileage. It's basically an insurance policy where you pay one lump sum for the contract to cover you for any major repairs less a deductible that you pay. Extended warranties may be transferable if purchased by the first owner and have not yet expired. Again, your dealer may get another sudden case of amnesia and fail to mention it in hope of selling you another one. Call the maker's zone office with the VIN of the car in question to find if a warranty exists.

As for paying the extra $500 to $900 in case something goes wrong, and then having to pay a deductible on top, you really only benefit when a catastrophe occurs, like an engine or transmission burns up. And that's not going to happen if it passes your mechanic's inspection and you follow my advice in the **Car Care** chapter. Your mechanic's inspection and my book are the best service contract you can buy, and they only cost about $50 and $10 respectively.

LEMON LAWS

Most states have by now adopted some kind of lemon law to protect the consumer. Although they only apply to people who have purchased new cars, I thought it might be worth mentioning here, in case you know of someone who got stuck with a lemon.

The State of California defines a lemon as any car that has been brought back to the manufacturer or dealership four or more times to fix the same problem unsuccessfully, or a car that has been out of service for more than 30 days. The four repair attempts or 30 days must have occurred within the first 12 months or 12,000 miles, whichever comes first. The problem must be covered by warranty and reduce the car's value, use, or safety, and not be caused by vehicle abuse. The consumer must also notify the manufacturer about the problem if so stated in the warranty or owner's manual.

If all these conditions are met by the consumer, the lemon law allows the buyer to a refund of the purchase price or a replacement vehicle, whichever the consumer prefers. For more information on California's State Lemon Laws call the Department of Consumer Affairs at 800-952-5210 for a free booklet on Lemon Laws. If you reside in another state, check with your state's Department of Consumer Affairs or check with your local librarian for more information.

ANOTHER WORD ON FINANCING

If you have excellent credit, there are times when the dealer can offer loan rates competitive with commercial banks and credit unions. If the finance person claims this, ask for their best possible rate. Even though you informed them you have outside financing, it is worthwhile to find out what they can offer.

When they ask what interest rate you've been approved for, just tell them you are locked in at a very competitive rate for X number of months and then ask again the best rate they can offer for the same number of months. Be sure not to tell them the rate you have secured. If you do, they will offer no more than 1/2% below yours, which may not be their lowest. But when they don't know your rate, you will be offered their lowest rate. Accept their loan only if it is a simple interest loan 1/2% lower or more (APR of course).

A word of caution: When financing through a dealer make sure the numbers are correct before you sign. The contract should show the loan percentage in Annual Percentage Rate. If they promise you a loan at 14.5% APR, then it must state 14.5% APR on the contract. The contract should also show the full amount of the loan, the cost of the loan, the monthly payments, and the number of months the term is for. Always read the entire contract before you sign, and if there is anything that you don't understand don't sign it until you do.

Also, make sure no blanks are left open. Blank spaces that don't apply should be filled with N/A for "not applicable". And find out up front if there are any prepayment penalties or processing fees. No one likes surprises. I recommend that you take the papers home with you so that you can take your time to read them over, rather than in a dealer's office with a salesman breathing down your neck.

THE EIGHT GOLDEN RULES FOR DEALING WITH DEALERS

1) Understand the way dealerships work
2) Have all your financing in order
3) Only shop reputable, new car dealership lots
4) Know all about the car(s) you seek
5) Take the car to your mechanic
6) Learn salesmen's tactics
7) Practice buyer's tactics
8) Never be in a hurry to buy from a dealer

IT'S HOW MUCH?!

CHAPTER 7:

DEALER NEGOTIATIONS

Probably the best way to learn shrewd negotiating is through observation. What follows are two fictional scenarios which place technique into action. To simplify things, the character in the first scenario is a single buyer with no car to trade in and no need for financing. This shows examples of how to negotiate when the dealer becomes tight because his only profit will come from the sale of his car.

In the second scenario we get more in depth with trade-in and financing techniques. Both offer various ways to handle salesman tactics. Before we get started though, a quick word on diplomacy.

YOUR APPROACH

Someone once said, "*Diplomacy is the art of letting someone else have your way.*" In other words, it's a polite way of winning someone over to your way of thinking. All good salesmen must have this talent if they are to be successful.

If you consider yourself diplomatic, you can certainly put it to good use here. Diplomacy is important in negotiating. You want to get the most car for the least amount of money without insulting or upsetting anyone in the process. If you do insult the salesman, you won't get as good a deal as you would have had you been diplomatic.

In using diplomacy during negotiating, you will be polite and respectful. Remember, they are pros at this and you are not, so respect them for it. You will also keep a positive attitude no matter how much of a scoundrel you think the salesman is. Don't call him a thief, crook, scumbag, or any of those other names that will enter your mind when negotiating. And don't call the car a piece of junk either. This will surely upset the salesman, and when that happens he gets really rigid in his negotiations. Besides, if the car really is a piece of junk then why are you in there trying to buy it?

As for honesty, it's not part of diplomacy. The dealer will be telling you plenty of fibs and you will be telling him your share of fibs. When you get right down to it, negotiating is a lot of B.S.'ing back and forth, and the one who comes out the winner is the one who was most creative.

NEGOTIATION SCENARIOS

If you ever wanted to be an actor, here is your chance for a starring role. The part you will be playing in the first act is that of Mr. Uninformed Buyer. However, by the second act your part will have evolved into a well-informed, shrewd negotiator. How much does this part pay, you ask? Anywhere from the low hundreds to well over a thousand dollars for one show. It all depends upon your experience and how well you can role play. The part involves thorough mental preparation, the ability to perform in front of a small live audience, and plenty of ad-libbing. Knowledge of the auto industry is helpful, but not required.

SCENARIO #1

Tony Johnson has shopped the lots and found a car he likes, and the sales manager allowed him to take the car to his mechanic for inspection. From his mechanic he discovered that the car will soon be needing front brakes and a new set of tires. Other than a cracked dash, a tear in the driver's seat, and a little oil seepage from under the valve cover, his mechanic came up with nothing seriously wrong. Overall the car is in good condition with an average number of miles on it.

Tony looked up the book value in *Edmunds* price guide to find it retailed at $5,075, while the dealer's sticker is a pricey $5,995. When Tony comes back to the lot with his mechanic's report and the retail book price, he just does what comes naturally.

[One quick note: Before you quote a book price to any dealer, don't forget to make the necessary add-ons or deductions. For example, a car with low miles you would add to the value, while a car with high miles you would deduct. Also, options like an automatic transmission or air- conditioning etc., will add to the book value. Make sure you understand how the price guide works completely or the dealer won't take you seriously if he sees that you forgot to add value for any options that the car may have.]

In this particular case, the car didn't have any added value.

Inside the sales office, Tony pitches his offer to "John," his salesman.

"Okay, John, we're looking at a car with a retail book of $5,075 and, according to my mechanic, will be needing brakes and tires soon and a new valve cover gasket pronto."

Now remember, this isn't coming off the top of his head. Tony has prepared himself for this pitch right after he received the mechanic's report. On paper he has figured in $300 for a set of tires, $100 for new front brakes and $45 for replacement of the gasket– $445 to be exact. But he doesn't stop there.

"And then we have that ugly dash that needs replacement and a front seat that needs to be reupholstered. Upholstery is expensive. Have you had anything upholstered lately, John?" Without giving him a chance to reply, Tony continues his pitch. "I called three upholsterers and the lowest quote I got was $250 for recovering the front seat and installing a new dash, but that didn't include the dash itself. That will run me another $125 bucks!"

Now, even though in the back of his mind Tony has already planned on a $40 seat cover and an $80 dash saver, he pitches the most costly method of correcting a flaw. This gives him an excuse to get the salesman to come down the maximum. Remember, John is going to come up with a bucket full of excuses to use against Tony, so it's always best to be creative and inflate problems as much as possible when you are negotiating.

Tony produces a list from his mechanic's report:

Book value	$5,075
Brakes	-100
Tires	-300
Valve gasket	-45
Dash	-125
Upholstery	-250
Adjusted total	**$4,255**

Tony goes over it with him.

"We have $5,075 retail book value on the car minus $100 for brakes, $300 for tires, etc., etc., bringing the new total to $4,255."

John looks at him and starts laughing, but it takes more than that to intimidate Tony. He looks at John dead serious.

"What's so funny, John? This is all valid, and I can back it up. Now, are you willing to work with me or are we just wasting each other's time?"

"Sure, I'll work with you, but there's really no way I could come down to a low-ball offer like that. I see where you are coming from, and I really sympathize with you, but there's just no way. We couldn't stay in business if we sold cars for less than we paid for them."

"I'm not asking you to sell it for less than you paid for it. All I'm asking for is some fair compensation, John."

John leans back in his chair.

"Look, you can't just knock $900 off the price just because of what some price guide says. The dealer's Blue Book retail price for that car is over $6,000. This car is well worth the asking price. Why, just last week I sold one like it for $200 more."

Tony knows that the "we just sold one like it for more money" line is B.S. If they sold one for more money then why is this one priced for less?

"John, what are you talking about? The Blue Book is over-inflated to begin with. *Edmunds Used Car Price Guide* is more accurate, and I just happen to have one with me." Tony pulls the book from his pocket. "The retail price quoted in *Edmunds* is $5,075 and your price is $5,995, almost a thousand above book. I would say that's a bit out of the ball park, wouldn't you?" Tony says.

"*Edmunds* is just a price guide and nothing more. The real world works by supply and demand, my friend, and these particular models happen to be in high demand. After all, they have one of the best repair records," John says.

"Are you trying to tell me that you don't mark up the prices to give yourselves room to negotiate?"

John still refuses to budge.

"All our cars are priced at fair market value."

Now Tony gives him his first ultimatum.

"All your cars are priced hundreds above market value, John. Now come on. Are you going to start price adjusting, or am I going to buy a car somewhere else?"

Tony acts upset, like he's about to get up. John bends for the first time.

"Okay, look, let me run it by my manager and see what he says. If I can get it for you at $5,750 will you buy the car today?"

Tony is well prepared for the "If I could..." line.

"I tell you what, John. If you can get him to lower it to $5,500, I will continue further negotiations to close this deal."

John gets up not liking his answer. Tony grabs him before he leaves.

"If you're not back in five minutes, I'll assume the deal fell through."

John acknowledges and exits. Tony figures John will call his bluff and not show up within five minutes. To counteract John's delay-of-game tactic, Tony goes out to the showroom and walks around like he's deep in thought. A few minutes later, John finds him.

"I have some good news, Mr. Johnson. Shall we go back to my office?" John leads Tony back to his office for the "good news."

"You are very smart for wanting one of these cars. They have one of the best reliability ratings in the used car market. And being highly rated puts them in very high demand. We have a hard time keeping them on our lot. So if you don't buy this car today, we are confident that we will have it sold by the end of the week to someone else. Yet, because you are prepared to buy today, my manager will knock off $250, which is more than halfway between $5,500 and $5,995. So, what do you say? Do we have a deal?"

The salesman has backed Tony into a corner using the urgency tactic. Tony is aware that the car he wants is highly rated, and they could very well be selling like hotcakes. Tony must do some quick thinking and change his approach. He pulls his calculator out of his pocket.

[By the way, having a pocket calculator with you is handy. It gives you an authoritive command. Instead of having to trust the salesman's calculations, he can only confirm yours. So be sure to bring one along.]

The other half of the difference between $5,500 and $5,995 is $245 which Tony adds to his work sheet figure of $4,255. He comes up with $4,500.

"Okay, John, I understand what you are saying. If I don't buy the car from you, someone else will. Maybe you will sell it by the weekend, but then again, maybe you won't. Is that a risk your manager is willing to take? I am here today ready to buy the car from you if you are willing to be fair about it. I think it would be very foolish on your manager's part if he refuses to work with me. Now my initial offer was $4,244 and because you agreed to come down $250, I will meet you by coming up $245 which is the other half of the $495 book price issue. That brings my new total to $4,500. Considering all the problems with the car, I think that's a fair offer. After all, the next person who looks at it, whenever that may be, will find the same flaws I have."

John is amazed how Tony danced his way around the urgency tactic.

"Look, I already told you I can't let this car go for less than we paid for it."

Tony continues haggling.

"What are you talking about, John? I just added $245 to my first offer. I think I'm being very flexible. Now what about the rest of these. We have $820 in repairs here. What do you want to do? You want to put on a new set of tires for me? If so, we can just scratch that $300 deduction right off the list!"

Using his mechanic's report, Tony has turned the tables on him. Instead of the salesman trying to talk Tony up in price, he has to talk him down on the repair costs.

"Why should we replace the tires? The ones that are on there are fine."

"Why should I buy a car that will need new tires in two months when I can go down the street and buy a used car with brand new tires for the same price?"

John shakes his head, frustrated.

"Okay, let me talk to my manager. He's going to think I'm nuts. If I can compensate you for the tires will you buy the car today?

Again, Tony is prepared.

"If he compensates me for the tires, I will continue my negotiations and try hard to close this deal with you."

John was afraid he would say something like that. He exits. Tony waits a good five minutes and then decides it's time for a refreshment. He finds himself a soda machine and gets a drink. The sales manager will likely see that John has a tough customer on his hands. Tony figures it's only a matter of time until the sales manager shows his face to do some haggling himself. John shows up at the vending machine with a big smile. Tony acknowledges him.

"What's the story, John?

"My manager really wants to make this work. Shall we go back to my office?"

Back in his office John gives him the lowdown.

"He's going to let me pro-rate them. First of all, your price on a set of tires is a little high. We know of a tire shop right down the street where you can get a set of four new tires for $200."

Tony is on his toes.

"I don't want retreads, John."

"These aren't retreads, they're brand name tires."

"Don't forget to add for balancing and sales tax. That can bring it up another $50. To be fair we should figure them to cost $250."

"Boy, you don't miss a beat, do you? Okay, the current tires are a 20,000-mile tire and with 5,000 miles left means you have 1/4th life left on them."

Tony does his own calculating to double check what John is figuring. Twenty-five percent of $250 is $62.50 which he then deducts. This amounts to $187.50. Not bad for tires he won't need to replace for another 5,000 miles. Match this with the $250 from the book price and so far he has talked John down $437.50. That's a nice chunk of change for less than an hour's worth of work. John looks at him with a big smile.

"Okay, you were a tough one. The car is yours for $5,557.50. I'll start writing this up right now. Are you ready to drive home in your new sedan?"

But when Tony checks his figures where he added $187.50 to $4,500, he came up with $4,687.50. At $5,557 the car is still way above the book value. Tony has some more hard bargaining to do.

"Wait a minute, not so fast. Were you going to just forget about the rest of these things on my list? John, I'm surprised at you."

John sighs.

"I'm sorry, but we're really at the bottom now. You just came in here and had your way with us."

A line like this is pure B.S. He's trying to make Tony sound victorious, like he already won the fight and it's over. Tony figures there's lots more room left for haggling.

"Come on, John, what about these brakes. I know they're not covered under warranty. Either install some new brakes or knock off another hundred bucks."

"First of all, the brakes that are on there are fine. Our mechanics check everything over thoroughly. We wouldn't sell a car that wasn't safe. Second of all, even if it did need new front brakes, you could get them done for a lot less than a hundred dollars."

"Well there you go, John. Why don't you just put them on if they're so cheap?"

This is where Tony needs to be careful. John might promise new brakes and scribble a quick note on the contract saying so, but when it comes time for the free service he may find John wasn't authorized. When a salesman starts scribbling promises on the contract, it's time to bring in the sales manager for approval. Should they agree to provide new brakes, Tony will demand they be installed before he takes the car or they can accept his $100 deduction.

"Okay, look, I'll compensate you fifty bucks for the brakes, but that's the very bottom I can go on this car. Now let's wrap up this deal."

Now John's at $5,507.50 and Tony comes up $50 more to $4,737.50.

"Okay. So that means you're going to have the dash and seat fixed for me? You must have friends in the upholstery business."

"No, we don't. This is the best we can do. You can't expect to get a six-year-old car and still have it in perfect condition. There will always be little things wrong.

Tony goes for broke.

"Okay, I tell you what. I'm at $4,737.50 and you're at $5,507.50. To sweeten the deal, I'm prepared to make you another offer. I'm really trying hard to make this deal work, John. However, if the deal falls through, it falls through. I'm sure I won't have much trouble finding another car with all the dealerships around. I'm going to offer you an even $4,800. I can write you a check out for the full amount. What do you say?"

John shakes his head no. "We couldn't possibly let it go for that," he says.

"How do you know? You haven't even asked your boss yet. Come on, John, work with me. Go talk to your manager."

John exits the office mumbling under his breath. Tony wonders if they will play the delay of game with him again. To no surprise, John's sales manager, "Kevin Greedy" shows up and introduces himself.

"John had to take an important call so he'll be a few minutes. Now, let's see what we have here." Kevin says, shuffling papers around.

"Did he tell you what my last offer was?" Tony asks.

"No." Kevin looks up, waiting to hear his offer.

"I'm offering $4,737.50 for your car and I can write you out a check for the full amount right now. How about it?" Tony asks. Tony took the opportunity to jump back to his previous offer to give himself more bargaining room. Kevin senses that he wants the car bad.

"Well, Mr. Johnson, we would like your business, but there's really no way we could accept a low-pitch offer like that. The price on our car is $5,995."

Tony smells a rat.

"Wait a minute, Kevin, John and I worked hard together to clear the price of $5,507 with you. Are you trying to tell me you are rescinding your offer? Because if that's the case, I'm going terminate this deal right now," Tony says, acting a bit angry.

"No, no. I never said that. I was merely pointing out how much we already came down."

"With a book retail of $5,075 and you being at $5,507, you really haven't come down at all. You are still high and making a killing. So my offer of $4,737.50 isn't a low-pitch offer at all when you think about it. Now, I know you pad your prices to give yourself negotiating room. There's nothing wrong with making a profit and succeeding in a business. I don't have a problem with that. You have bills to pay just like everyone else. But let's be fair about it, shall we? Now, I'm prepared to make you another offer to sweeten the deal. I will round off my offer to an even $4,800 which I can pay you today. Now I ask you, are you going to cut me a deal today or am I going to another dealership?"

Tony has given him an ultimatum. Kevin must drop the price or risk losing the sale. Tony is certain he can get him to go lower. If this car wasn't in such high demand he would be going for much lower stakes, but supply and demand does play a part in how much negotiation leeway you'll be granted. Kevin punches a few keys on his adding machine.

"Okay, the difference between $4,800 and $5,507 is $707. What do you say we split the difference? That would mean you can have the car for $5,153.50. That's a fair deal!"

Even if Tony was happy with the price and willing to buy it right now, he still continues to fight. He knows another twenty minutes of his time could save him hundreds more. Tony looks at him dead serious.

"No, I'm sorry. I can't do it. I tell you what, Kevin, I'm going to take a little break to give you time to think it over. I need to get the blood recirculating and use your restroom."

Tony gets up and exits. Even though Kevin figured him out earlier, Tony made it clear that he will walk if he doesn't get the deal he wants. Tony is certain he can get the car for $4,800 or very close to it. Tony takes his time in the restroom and takes a stroll through the showroom. After ten minutes of stalling, he goes back to the office to find it empty. Tony figures that maybe Kevin won't bend after all. As one last-ditch effort to get them to succumb, Tony heads for the door, making sure that he is seen.

He knows that after a couple of hours of negotiations, they just won't let him walk away. He figures if he makes it all the way to his car without getting chased down, Kevin really is at his lowest price. If it came to this Tony would go over the figures again to make sure this is what he wants and can afford. He can always walk back in and say he has reconsidered.

Once outside he finds John has followed him out.

"Oh, Mr. Johnson? We are prepared to give you the deal," he says.

It had worked. On the inside Tony is smiling from ear to ear, but on the outside he acts like it's no big deal. John leads him back to his office.

"Now, Mr. Johnson, Mr. Greedy says he will let you have the car for an even $4,900. I have already written up the contract. All you need to do is sign here and..."

"John, my offer was $4,800 for the car. Now a minute ago you said you were prepared to let me have the deal and the deal was for $4,800. Are you two getting your wires crossed again? Maybe you should go back and double check with him."

Frustrated, John leaves the room only to return a few minutes later.

"Okay, Tony, you win. $4,800 and not a penny less." John hands him the contract and Tony looks it over carefully and notices a $250 dealer prep fee.

"What's this?" Tony asks.

"That's a prep fee we charge on all trade-ins. It covers our mechanic's cost for tune-up and repairing whatever needs to be fixed and the detailing," John says casually.

"Well, I'm not paying a $250 prep fee on a car that needs new front brakes and has a leaking valve cover. Sounds to me like your prep fee is an excuse to add more profit to each deal. So you can either take it off or have the repairs done before I take it." Tony says.

Shaking his head, John exits the room and finds Kevin working in his office.

"He's not going to go for it, Mr. Greedy."

Kevin looks up. "You mean the extra charge?" John nods his head yes. Kevin sighs. "Okay, just wrap him up and get him out of here. I don't ever want to see his face again!" he says, disgusted with the meager $600 profit they will make off this deal.

SCENARIO #2

Paul and Lisa White are prepared to buy a car today. They know the exact model and features they want, have been pre-approved for a low interest loan with their credit union, and know the current value of their trade-in. They also have $2,000 in their checking account to use toward a down payment.

Two nights ago they shopped around and found just the car they were looking for, but it was priced $7,995, which is about $1,000 higher than they wanted to spend. After a test drive, they left the dealership with a salesman's offer of $300 below the listed price. Lisa scribbled $7,695 on the salesman's business card.

Earlier today, Paul went back to the dealership and drove the car to his mechanic for inspection. Although the car needs a front-end alignment and brakes, everything checked out fine. Paul dropped the car off at the dealer late in the afternoon and told the salesman he would get some dinner and be back with his wife later. Before he left, Paul found out how late they were open so they could plan on arriving about an hour and a half before they close.

The Whites know they are looking between two to three hours of negotiating with the sales staff. By getting there 90 minutes before closing, they plan to wear down and tire the salesman the same way salesmen do with most of their customers.

Paul and Lisa took a refreshing shower, ate a light dinner, and stopped off at a coffee house for a cappuccino and to plot their strategy. Not only are they are refreshed, they are mentally prepared as well. Their salesman, however, is near the end of a long day and is likely tired from a full day of sales babble.

After carefully looking the car over again and taking it for another test drive, they seemed concerned about the price. Tom, their salesman, reads them.

"Have you already sought outside financing?" Tom inquires.

Paul and Lisa are good actors and exchange an unsure look.

"Well, no," Lisa says.

"We were hoping that you could take care of it for us. You do offer financing, don't you?" Paul asks, playing dumb.

"We sure do. The best you'll find anywhere." Tom smiles, thinking about the extra commission he will make from their inflated rate. "Why don't we step inside and you can fill out a loan application. It will only take a few minutes."

Tom leads them into his office and hands them the loan app to fill out.

"I tell you what. While we are doing this why don't you have your guys check out our car." Paul tosses Tom the keys and points to his car through the window. "It's that baby right over there. Take her for a test drive if you like."

"Well, our manager needs to have you present when he checks over your vehicle," Tom says. Paul looks at him confused.

"That's okay, I trust you guys," Paul says, fibbing through his teeth.

"It's in case he has any questions," Tom adds.

"Don't worry about it," Paul insists. "If he has any questions he can ask me when he's through."

"Do you have your title with you?" Tom asks.

"Oh, yes. It should be in the glove box with the registration," Lisa says.

Lisa actually has their car's title and registration in her purse along with a spare set of keys just in case they try and pull the misplaced-keys-tactic.

Paul and Lisa finish with their loan app, and Tom strolls back in shortly after.

"So what did they think of our car?" Paul asks eagerly.

"My manager has been busy with other customers and didn't get a chance to look at it. Why don't we have a look at it now. He shouldn't be much longer." Tom gestures them toward the door.

Paul and Lisa know what will happen next. They will be forced to watch his manager go over every inch of their car, touching every flaw in front of them to set them up for the low-ball offer.

"Did you say the title was in the glove box? I didn't see it there," Tom inquires.

"Oh, I'm sorry. I have it right here. I forgot we were over at (name of competing dealership) and I had it out for them," Lisa says.

Lines like these precondition the salesman and do wonders for you at the negotiation table. For Tom this means he has some real shop-around buyers on his hands. He knows he can't be too stiff with his bargaining if he's to make a sale with Paul and Lisa or they will just head back to the other dealer tomorrow. Paul and Lisa know what's out there.

When they get out to their car, Tom's busy sales manager has miraculously broken away from the other customers. Tom introduces "Jack" to them. Just as they expected, Jack starts his silent inspection by touching a scratch on the fender. Paul and Lisa know to act unconcerned and to ignore as much as possible. Lisa pretends a nearby car has caught her eye and strolls over for a closer look, thwarting the manager's game.

"How much is this one going for, Tom?" she asks. Paul follows her lead.

"That looks like it will be a bit out of our range, hon," Paul says.

Annoyed, Tom tries to get their attention back. This is where Paul and Lisa get creative and disagree about some aspect of the pricey car, such as its color, etc. They get unhappy Tom to answer their questions.

Once Jack has finished his inspection he must check his books before he can make them an offer. Tom leads them back to his office, where the Whites inform Tom they don't like the price of his car.

"How much did you have in mind for a monthly payment?" he asks.

Lisa and Paul know to avoid this question. If they tell Tom what they want for a monthly payment, Tom can easily calculate a way for them to afford their desired car by either stretching the loan term or increasing the down payment or a combination of both. Of course, this will be figured at the maximum profit for the dealership. With a quick juggling of figures it's easy to twist things around to make it appear you are getting a good deal.

Worse yet, the Whites will be forced into negotiating the sale of the car by adjusting the monthly payments, which is not a fair method of negotiation for the buyer. Dealers sell many cars this very way without the buyer ever knowing the actual amount of the purchase price. The salesman tries to hook them with the low-monthly-payment carrot. Fortunately, Paul and Lisa are hip to this.

"We aren't worried about monthly payments as much as we are about the price of the car," Lisa says.

Even though monthly payments are a main concern for Paul and Lisa, they already know how much car they can afford through their pre-approved loan from their credit union. They also know exactly what their monthly payments will be if they stay within their predetermined limit. Although the car they have targeted is $1,000 above that, they are confident that they can get very close to their goal through negotiating.

"Tell me what you can afford. What's the most you are comfortable with? If I could, say, get you in at $350 a month, would you take the car tonight?" Tom persists.

"The issue here isn't what we can or cannot afford in terms of monthly payments. The issue is what price we are willing to pay for this car," Paul asserts. "If you want to sell us this car tonight, you'll have to negotiate in terms of the total price of the car. Once we agree on a price for your car and the trade-in value for our car, then we can figure out our payments."

This is nicely put. Tom is annoyed because his favorite selling ploy has been nullified. But he's not worried. He has plenty more.

"So what did you have in mind for a price?"

Paul knows to avoid making the first offer, whether it's for his trade-in or the car they want. The person who makes the first offer loses an edge by taking that risk of testing the bargaining waters. Offer too low, the dealer scoffs at you. Offer too much and your dollars are flying out the window. Do everything possible to get him to make the first offer in both cases.

"Well, we're still wondering what you're going to offer us on our trade-in. Shouldn't we figure that out first?" he asks.

"Yeah, what's taking him so long to decide?" Lisa adds.

"He has to look it up in the books and make all those considerations. You can't just come up with a figure off the top of your head, you know."

"How long does it take to look it up and decide? Why don't you check with him," Paul insists.

Tom agrees and goes to his sales manager. Even though it may be safe to talk after Tom leaves the office, Paul and Lisa know not to discuss their target prices or strategies. Sales offices have been known to be bugged and they aren't taking any chances. Inside the office they engage in small talk. If they need to discuss figures, they go outside the office. Leaving the office for a soda or a stroll around the showroom always brings the salesman back quicker.

Tom finds the Whites out in the showroom.

"Good news. Jack is in a generous mood tonight and has made a better offer than I would have thought," Tom says.

Lisa's eyes light up. "How much?"

"Why don't we go back to my office where we can sit down and discuss it." Tom leads them back to his office for the "good" news.

"What's the good news?" Paul asks.

"We will give you $800 for your trade, which would cut the $7,995 price down to $7,195. Now, on an '89 that's a good deal."

Paul and Lisa exchange another one of their confused looks.

"But I don't understand. Our car is worth much more than that," Paul says.

"Not with that dent in the fender and the engine leaking oil like it is."

"The fender isn't dented. It's just a scratch," Paul says, defending his car.

"Our car doesn't leak oil," Lisa insists.

"Yes, your car is leaking oil from behind the rear main seal. Do you know how much it costs to replace a main seal?" Tom says as if it was a $5000 job. Paul and Lisa have no idea what a rear main seal is, let alone how much it costs to replace it. They do know, however, that their car hasn't leaked oil before tonight or they would have noticed the drops on their clean garage floor. This is news to them. Could it have just started, or is the salesman just making up a story to use to his advantage. Paul figures the salesman is B.S.'ing them, but that's okay because Paul and Lisa have no intention of trading in their car anyway.

"So I guess that means he won't go up anymore for us on that?" Paul asks.

"Not with the problems it has."

Paul looks at Lisa and she gives a shrug and a nod.

"Okay, that means we're looking at $7,195 minus $300 is $6,895."

"$300? Where did the $300 come from?" Tom asks.

"From you two nights ago." Paul produces Tom's business card with the quote written on it. "Remember? You're not going back on what you said, are you?"

"Oh, that was with the assumption that you were going to buy the car outright."

"What does it matter if we buy it outright or if we finance, you'll still get paid."

"Okay, I tell you what. I'll run it by Jack and see what he says. If I can get him to approve it will you take the car tonight?" Tom asks.

"We'll figure that out when you get back," Lisa says.

Again Tom goes back to his manager and the Whites head for the soda machine where they discuss their next strategy. Paul and Lisa don't want to pay more than $7,000 for their next car. They know that it is quite common for dealers to mark up their used cars anywhere from 20% to 25%. This means the dealer likely gave a trade allowance between $6,000 and $6,400 for the $7,995 car.

Even though the Whites' trade-in has brought the price down below $7,000, in the end they won't be trading in their car and will have to add this amount back onto the price. So in Paul's and Lisa's minds the car is still at $7,695 and they need to bargain off another $695. Obviously, they have some haggling left to do.

After about ten minutes, they mosey around the showroom to get the attention of either Tom or Jack.

Back in the office Tom presents them with a contract.

"Okay, you win. Jack is going to let you have the car for $6,895 plus your trade." Tom pushes the contract towards them. Paul and Lisa exchange a look.

"We never said we'd take it at that price, Tom. We are definitely interested in the car, but only if the price is right," Paul says.

Tom looks him dead in the eye. "Look, you're getting a great deal on this. We couldn't possibly go any lower. We have to make some profit to survive. We have to eat, too, you know." Tom nods to the photos of his wife and kids displayed prominently on the desk. His timing was perfect. But Paul doesn't go for the guilt trip.

"Well, we don't have a problem with that, Tom. We expect you to make a profit. We just want it to be fair for both sides. We have kids too, and times are tough. Believe me, we know what it's like. Now, we both have a lot of respect for you and your dealership. We have friends who bought here in the past and were very pleased with their car and the service they received. They especially raved about how Jack was willing to go out of his way for their business. So, like I said before, we are interested in buying this car tonight but only if the price is right," Paul says.

"The price is right!" Tom says.

Paul turns to Lisa who produces a mechanic's report from her purse.

"Our mechanic looked over the car and found it to be in pretty good shape, except it will be needing brakes soon and the front end is out of alignment. His estimate is $250 for the brakes and another $50 for the alignment. When it is all said and done it amounts to over $300 with tax. Now, if Jack is willing to compensate us for this, we would still be interested in making a purchase tonight," Paul says.

"Wait a minute, let's back up a bit here. Our price for the car from the start was $7,995 and so far we have gone down to $6,895 to accommodate you. That's $1,100. We have compensated as much as we can."

"The trade-in allowance is irrelevant, Tom. That's a separate deal which you will make another profit on. And the $300 that you knocked off was an offer that you made to us before we even started negotiating. So the way we look at it $6,895 is just the starting point for negotiating. We are really counting on you to help us close this deal. Go ask Jack to compensate us the $300 for the brakes and alignment," Paul says. Tom looks at him, shaking his head.

"He's going to think I'm crazy," Tom mumbles as he heads out the door.

Paul and Lisa again walk out of the office to discuss their strategy. Lisa checks her watch and it's 9:45pm--45 minutes after closing. Hopefully, Tom and Jack will start getting frustrated and give in soon. She just wants to go home in their new car. Unfortunately, the salesmen are using the same strategy on them. After 15 minutes go by, Jack shows up.

"Tom had to take an important call and may be tied up for a few minutes. Why don't we go back to his office and see where we are." Jack leads them back to Tom's office.

Now, Paul and Lisa know that when there is a turnover from a salesman to the manager, they have been tight negotiators. This means that Tom was running out of steam and Jack is moving in to do the clean-up. He will most likely go over all the same points, but from a different angle.

When Jack tries the monthly payment game, Paul and Lisa forcefully tell him, just as they told Tom, that they only negotiate through the price of the dealer's car and their trade-in. Jack changes gears.

"Okay. We are willing to give you $800 on your trade-in, which is being very generous. With the number of miles on that car and all its problems we will just have to wholesale it out to an auction company. We are not going to make any money on your trade, which means we need to make a few dollars on our car. Now, our price started out at $7,995 and we have knocked off $800 for your trade and another $300 which Tom promised you, which he isn't authorized to do, no less, but he's my employee so I can't take back what he promised. Now that adds up to $1,100 in deductions and brings the price down to $6,895. And at that price, believe me, you are getting one good deal. Tom has already drawn up a contract. You do have something for a down payment, I presume?"

"How much would you need?" Paul asks.

"Fifteen hundred would be nice."

"That isn't a problem," Lisa says, "but the price you want for this car is."

"As you know, we had our mechanic check it out and he found the front end out of alignment and the car will soon need brakes all the way around," Paul adds. "Now don't get me wrong. We like the car, and we are ready to buy tonight, but only if the price is what we think is fair."

"And what to you think is fair?" Jack asks.

"Well, first we want to know if you're going to compensate us for the brakes and alignment, or are we going back to (competing dealer down the street) where the sales staff will bend over backward for our business," Paul says.

Jack stares for a moment with a smirk on his face. Paul and Lisa can tell he's an unhappy camper.

"Okay, tell you what I can do. I'll have the alignment checked over by our mechanic and knock off another hundred dollars for the brakes. What do you say?"

Paul realizes that having the "alignment checked over" doesn't mean anything.

"Have the alignment checked over? We don't need it checked over. We already know it's whacked. We need it fixed!" Paul barks.

"Now honey, calm down," Lisa says.

Paul acts very upset. Maybe he really is or maybe he's just acting it up a little bit. Paul knows that acting upset in front of the salesman will usually get them to bend. They will fear losing you if they don't give in to something.

"Okay, we'll fix it. We will fix the alignment," Jack says.

"We would like that in writing on the contract, if you don't mind," Lisa adds.

"That's no problem," Jack says.

"Now, what about the brakes? Our mechanic gave an estimate of $250. A $100 isn't going to cut it," Paul says.

"But the brakes on there are fine. Why should we compensate you for full price when you may get another ten, fifteen thousand miles on them?" Jack asks.

"Our mechanic told us soon, which may be next month. The way we see it, the car needs brakes now. But because we are willing to bend to make this deal fly, and it is getting late..."

"That it is," Jack adds.

"Just deduct an even $200 instead of the $250. That should more than make up for whatever life is left on the brakes," Paul says.

"All right. A deal is a deal. Take the car for $6,695 plus your trade-in. I'll go have Tom write it up," Jack says, offering his hand to Paul for a shake.

"Wait a minute. I never said I would buy it for that. We still have some negotiating left to do," Paul says.

"Mr. White, please, be reasonable. We couldn't possibly go any lower in price. We are barely making any money as it is. We have to pay bills too, you know," Jack says.

"I know, I know. I don't have a problem with that. We know you need to make a living and we also know you make that living by selling cars. On some cars you make a huge profit and on some you make a marginal profit. It all balances out over the long run, right? So it is well worth it for you to move cars as fast as possible. Now, we are willing to write a check right now for $2,000 as a down payment if you let us take the car for an even $6,000 plus our trade-in. We would finance the rest through you, of course. How about it?" Paul asks after his beautifully prepared speech.

"I'm sorry, Mr. White, we just can't do it for that low of a price. That's way below book," Jack says. Paul gestures to Lisa. They both stand up.

"We need a break. Why don't you take a minute to think it over, Jack. We're going to grab a soda real quick and be back in a few minutes."

Jack acknowledges with a wave as the two exit the office. Out at the soda machine Lisa notices it's 10:15 now. She and Paul are stressed from all the haggling, but they feel they have made progress and are very close to closing the deal. They both look forward to leaving in their new car. They notice Jack walking by, not looking very happy.

About ten minutes later Jack shows up.

"Are you guys ready to close this deal?" he asks.

"That all depends on you," Paul says. They all stroll back to the office.

"So, did you have a chance to think it over?" Paul asks.

"Yes, and if you want to make this work you're going to have to do better than that," he says.

"Wait a minute, I made you the offer of $6,000 last. If you don't want to accept that, then it's your turn to come back with a counteroffer. That's the way negotiation works, at least in my book," Paul says.

Jack sighs. It's clear that he's tired and frustrated. He'd rather be home.

"Okay, look, I really want this deal to work. I'll take another hundred dollars off, but that's it and not a dollar more. You can have the car for $6,595 plus your trade and that, Mr. White, is the best I can do," Jack says forcefully.

Paul and Lisa exchange a look. Is that the best he can really do, or is he just holding out? They both wonder if they pushed him to his limit. $6,595 plus the $800 for their trade means they would essentially be paying $7,395 for the car which is $395 more than they want to. That means they only talked him down $600; a respectable sum, but it's still above book value. Paul decides to forego the dealer's warranty in lieu of more cash discount.

"I tell you what, Jack, this car comes with a warranty, right?" Paul asks.

"That's correct."

"And that warranty has to be worth something, right?" Paul continues.

"Of course," Jack says.

"I thought so too. Why don't you keep your warranty and let me take the car for $6,000 plus my trade. Think of it this way: you'll never have to see my face in here again," Paul says jokingly. Jack smirks as if he likes the sound of that.

Because Paul took the car by his mechanic earlier in the day, he knows the car's mechanically sound and will unlikely need anything throughout the warranty term. Therefore, why pay for something that he won't use? Paul's trip to the mechanic is his warranty, and a much better deal for the price.

"When people want to go without a warranty, the best I can do is to discount another $100 off the price," Jack says.

"Your warranty is only worth a hundred bucks?"

"You can't put a price on a warranty, Mr. White. You will probably never need it, but it's there as a safety net, so to speak. If you are willing to take that risk, then I can discount you another hundred bucks and not a penny more," Jack says.

Paul makes the simple subtraction on his calculator. "That brings us down to $6,495, Jack. We're only $495 apart!" Paul laughs, but Jack doesn't.

It's late and everyone wants to finish this up and go home. Paul thinks that maybe Jack is truly at his bottom and, considering that the car is now theirs for $7,295 ($6,495 plus the $800 for their trade), they have brought the price down to within $295 of their goal. Paul and Lisa excuse themselves to have a conference.

Outside the office and out of sight of Jack, they quietly agree that the price of $7,295 is acceptable to them, but before they give in Paul will try one last round of dickering just to make sure that, indeed, Jack is at his bottom. They re-enter the sales office, not smiling, but rather, looking very stern.

"Okay, we talked about it and this is what we are willing to do. Considering that we are only $495 apart, we will meet you halfway at $6,250 plus our trade and you keep your warranty. Come on Jack, what do you say? Let's close this deal and go home," Paul says.

"I already told you I can't go any lower, Mr. White. We would be losing money at that price," Jack claims.

"Why don't you just let us have the car for $6,250? You can make it up on your next sale. Come on, Jack."

"Mr. and Mrs. White, let me explain something to you. We have to make a certain percentage on each car that we sell just to cover overhead. This car that you have bargained us down to $6,495 is right at that overhead cost now. If I go any lower we lose money," Jack says.

"But if you add the $800 for our trade to that, we are really paying $7,295 for your car, which is still above book, and then you're getting our trade, which will give you another profit," Paul pleads.

"I told you before that your trade-in isn't going to make us any profit. We'll have to wholesale it out to an auction just to get rid of it. We are doing you a favor by taking it off your hands at $800," Jack says, getting frustrated.

Paul knows this is a line of B.S. Even though his car isn't perfect, he knows it's worth between $2,500 and $3,000. Jack is going to make a killing on it and then has the nerve to say he is doing them a favor? It won't bother Paul one bit when he suddenly changes his mind about trading in their car.

"I tell you what, Jack, I'll give you our final offer of $6,300 plus our trade and you keep your warranty. Now, we have come up $300 and you only need to come down $195. We are really trying to close this deal with you, and I think this offer is being very fair to you." Jack looks at Paul like he's the customer from hell. "Come on, Jack, what's another $195?" Paul adds.

Jack looks at his watch and starts laughing. "You just never quit, do you?" Paul smiles. "Considering that it's very late and I'm very tired, I'm going to succumb to your offer of $6,300. Let me find Tom, and he'll go through the paper work with you."

"Don't forget about fixing the alignment. We'd like that in writing, please," says Lisa who seems to have come alive now that they have made progress. Jack acknowledges and leads them to the closing office and leaves them. A moment later their old buddy Tom shows up with a bunch of papers.

"You made it! Congratulations! I heard you were pretty tough on him in there," he says.

"He was pretty tough on us!" Paul claims.

"We're really sorry about keeping you here so late," Lisa says.

"Don't worry about it. I'm used to it by now... Okay, before we finalize I want to go over a couple of things really quick," Tom says.

"If it's about an extended warranty we're not interested," Paul says.

"We already gave up our warranty that came with the car," Lisa adds.

"This is actually a service contract and buying your car without a warranty is all the more reason to consider this. It covers any defects with your engine or drive train for two years with only a $100 deductible. Your timing is good because normally it's $600, but this month we are running a special on it for only $495." Tom does a couple of quick calculations on his computer and looks up, "It would only be another seventeen dollars a month."

"Tom, why would we cash in a measly $100 for your dealership's warranty and then pay $495 for this one?" Paul asks.

"Because this is much more thorough coverage. What if you developed a transmission leak and burned up your transmission? Do you know how much that can cost?" Tom says, trying to sell them on their fears.

Paul and Lisa exchange a look. They know what he is trying to do.

"Pass!" They both say.

After trying to sell them a car alarm, fabric protection treatment, and rustproofing, of all things, Tom reaches the end of his list of extras unsuccessfully. He reluctantly prepares the final paperwork when he notices Lisa seems to need to say something to Paul.

"Will you excuse us just a second?" Paul says as he and Lisa stand up.

"Sure," Tom says.

They exit the office and have a make-believe conversation. This is where they are going to change their mind about their trade-in. After a couple of minutes they re-enter.

"We changed our minds," Paul says.

"What!?" Tom says in disbelief.

"Don't worry, Tom, we still want the car; we just decided to keep our trade, that's all," Paul says.

"We almost forgot about our nephew who's in need of a car," Lisa adds.

"So add the $800 to the price and make it $7,100. Our credit is good for it," Paul says.

Tom's mouth drops open. "Mr. White, I'm afraid I can't do that."

"What? Why not?" Paul asks.

"Because we had an agreement already worked out with your trade-in."

"But that was for $800 and now we are giving you that $800 in the loan amount. Jack told us over and over how our trade wasn't going to make him any money anyway. He was just going to wholesale it out to an auction. So what do you care if we change our minds? You should be happy that you're getting $800 more," Paul says.

Tom jumps up and excuses himself. He has to let Jack know what's going on. After a few minutes Jack steps in.

"What seems to be the problem?" he asks.

"No problem, Jack. We just decided to keep our trade-in, that's all," Paul says.

"Actually we had forgotten about our nephew who needs a car," Lisa adds.

"But we had already agreed on the trade," Jack says.

"What difference does it make? I thought you'd be happy about this. You're the one who kept telling us that you were going to wholesale it to an auction at no profit. Instead, we're giving you $800 dollars more for your car. Why the hesitation?" Paul asks.

Jack seems to be at a loss for words. Paul and Lisa knew his story was a bunch of bull. He was going to sell it from his lot and make a huge profit.

"Well, it just makes it inconvenient having to rewrite the paperwork and all."

"That's okay, Jack. Just scratch out the figures, make the changes, and initial them. You didn't forget about including the alignment repair, did you?" Paul asks. Jack wants to pull the hair out of his head. He excuses himself. Momentarily, Tom shows up with a new contract and proceeds to cover the points.

"Okay, with $7,100 for the price of the car plus tax, license, and dealer prep fees brings the total to..."

"Wait a minute. What's this $150 charge for?" Paul asks, pointing to the contract.

"That's the dealer prep charge for preparing the car for sale. All our cars are subject to this fee," Tom says.

"Tom, we're not paying a $150 for a car wash. Take it off. When we negotiated a price for this car, aside from the tax and licensing, we were under the assumption that all those fees were included. I'm sorry, but you'll have to eat that one," Paul says forcefully as if the fate of the deal hinged upon the prep fee.

Being this far into the closing, Paul would only pay it if it was necessary to save the deal. But instead of readily paying it, Paul pretends to jeopardize the deal by refusing to pay the phony prep fee. No dealer will allow a sale to fall through after having all this time invested. They will remove the fee. But in the unlikely event that they do refuse after you threaten to walk out, you can simply reconsider. It costs you nothing to try and your efforts can result in hundreds saved.

Tom excuses himself to go clear it with Jack who, Paul figures, will be steaming by now. He wonders how he will run the financing change by. He may just have to take their high-interest loan and then pay it off in full with their lower interest loan from their credit union; that is, if the dealer's loan doesn't have stiff prepayment penalties.

Tom re-enters with the news that he was allowed to take off the prep fee. Tom starts going over the loan terms while Paul is plotting in his mind how he should break this to him. He certainly doesn't want the deal to fall through because of their sudden change of mind in financing. When Tom gets to the part about interest rate, Paul decides to test the waters.

"Wait a minute stop right there. Did you say 15% APR?" Paul asks.

"Yes, and at 36 months that comes to..." Tom tries to brush it off.

"I thought you quoted us 13% earlier. What happened?" Paul asks.

"I never quoted you that. I told you 15% right from the beginning," Tom says.

"Where am I getting 13 % from?" he looks at his wife.

"I think I mentioned our bank was offering loans at 13%, hon," Lisa says.

"Well, if that's the case I think we should get a loan from our own bank, don't you?" Paul looks at Lisa.

"Definitely," she adds.

"Mr. and Mrs. White, you had already agreed to our terms for financing. Breaking that agreement would be in violation of our contract," Tom says.

"What contract? We never signed anything," Paul says.

"We're sorry about changing our minds again, but we misunderstood a crucial point about the loan," Lisa says. Tom is clearly upset.

"Look, just give us 48 hours to see if we can qualify. If we don't, we'll take your loan as it stands. Here's a check for $2,000 for the down payment. We'd like to take the car tonight. Is that a problem?" Paul asks.

Tom is fuming under his collar. He jumps up and excuses himself again. Paul and Lisa realize that this might not fly with Jack, especially after stripping him of the profit he was counting on from their trade-in. The dealer loan was the last avenue for any extra profits they could possibly make. But if Jack refuses to accept their outside financing, Paul and Lisa have another option. They can always accept the dealer loan and then turn around and pay it off in full through their credit union's lower interest loan. As long as there isn't a stiff pre-payment penalty on the dealer loan, this is another great way to save money.

Tom comes back.

"I'm afraid we can't let you do that. Not after our agreement," Tom says.

"But we never signed anything," Lisa says.

"It doesn't matter. We had an oral agreement," Tom says. Paul suspects they may be bluffing. He figures if they threaten to walk out, Tom and Jack will reconsider. But before he goes to this extreme, he decides to have a look at the loan contract. He skims through it looking for information about prepayment penalties. These are penalties the loan company will charge should you happen to pay the loan off early.

Paul finds the information he was looking for; there's no prepayment penalty. Now they can accept the loan and turn around and pay it off with a lower interest loan from their credit union.

Paul looks at Lisa and nods. "Okay, if we have to, we have to. Where do we sign?"

Tom is relieved that they didn't call their bluff. Jack is already upset with him enough as it is. Tom shows Paul where to sign on the loan agreement. Paul takes the contract and reads through it carefully, making sure everything is correct. He then hands it to Lisa, who double checks everything.

With tax, licensing, smog, and documentary fees, the total price of the car would be $7,783.75. Minus their $2,000 down payment, the loan amount would be $5,783.75. With a 36-month term at 15% APR the payments will be $200.49 per month. Although their payments at 13% would be $194.88, $5.61 less, that would add up to $201.96 in savings over the term of the loan. Their credit union charges a $60 documentation fee for their auto loan, which means they will save $141.96, thus making it worthwhile to switch.

When checking over the loan document, Lisa knows it is important that no blank spaces are left open. If there are blank spaces that don't apply, she fills in "N/A" for "not applicable". Lisa finishes and nods her approval to Paul. Just before they sign, Paul asks which copy is theirs.

"The bottom yellow copy is yours," Tom says.

The Whites know it's important that they get a copy of the contract right after signing it and not later that night or the next day. Some shady dealers will try to tell you otherwise so they can take the contract and alter the interest rate, etc. So get a copy of everything you sign immediately.

The next contract is for their car. Lisa double checks it after Paul. "I don't see anything about having the alignment fixed," she says. Paul was so wrapped up in the loan figures he'd forgotten about it. He's thankful that she remembered.

"We have a special service contract that we've written up for that," Tom says showing her the document.

"I'd still like to see it on our original contract as well. Is that a problem?" She asks

"No," he says.

"Why don't you just hand write it in somewhere that it's included in the price and have Jack initial it. That should be fine," Paul says.

"I know there's no one in the service department this late, but would you have any idea when we could bring it by to have the alignment corrected?" Lisa asks.

"You'd have to call the service department and find out from them, Mrs. White. I know they are busy this time of year so it may take a week or two. I would call them first thing in the morning and set up an appointment," Tom says.

"That sounds like a good idea," Paul adds.

Now with the contract in front of them, Paul and Lisa confirm the selling price of their new car along with the down payment and the total amount of the loan they are paying. They also make sure that any details on the contract that are not applicable are filled in with N/A. They both sign and get a copy.

Paul and Lisa also sign the little service claim check that will allow for the repair on their car. They all stand up and shake hands. Tom is relieved that this transaction is over. He just wants these two out of his hair. Never has he made such a small commission in his life, and he hopes this will be the last.

A FEW LAST TIPS

•Timing can play a part in getting a better deal on a car. The end of the day, the end of the week, the end of the month, and the end of the year are the best times to make a purchase. This means the optimum time to purchase a car would be right around New Year's Eve. Of course, not everyone can wait until then, but do try holding out for the end of the month. Most dealerships have certain sales goals they try to meet for each month, and when they fall short, they become eager to make a sale at this time.

•Always try to hook up with the youngest salesman on the lot. He will be less experienced at car selling and, because he is new, will be more concerned with selling a car to prove himself to his boss, and less concerned with making a huge profit.

•Never fear the salesman or sales manager. They may be pros in the auto industry, but they are just as human as you. At the same time, don't get on too personal a level with them either. They will do their best to become your friend, so later you feel sorry for them and give in to their price. Keep them at a professional distance.

•Repetition works, I tell you. Repetition works, I tell you. Don't hesitate to repeat yourself frequently during negotiations. Saying the same thing, but rewording each time, works best.

THE SIX GOLDEN RULES OF DEALER NEGOTIATIONS

1) Always be polite and respectful
2) Save your actual car buying for the end of the month
3) Bargain, bargain, bargain
4) Watch for phony dealer add-ons
5) Don't sign any contract without completely reading and fully understanding it
6) Never be in a hurry to buy from a dealer

PART III:

HOW TO SELL AND CARE FOR YOUR USED CAR

CHAPTER 8:

SELLING YOUR USED CAR

This book wouldn't be complete if I didn't include a chapter on how to sell your car. In the following chapter I offer some great advice designed to help you sell your car quickly, and for its maximum worth. Even if you don't have a car to sell you should consider reading this chapter because it will put you in the seller's shoes and give you a different point of view.

Why are you selling your car? That's the most important thing to ask when you call about a car and, undoubtedly, will be asked of you when you go to sell yours. So you better be prepared.

Why *are* you selling your car? If you are selling your car because it's a lemon, I'm not for burning people. That's not what this book is about. Even though you got burned on the deal, tighten up your belt one more notch and accept the loss. Sell your lemon for whatever it's worth and chock it up to experience. And, by the way, you probably wouldn't want to sell it to a friend or an acquaintance. If the car was a problem for you, it will be a problem for them, so you won't be winning any popularity contests from whoever buys it.

Let's consider the real reasons people sell their cars:

Reason #1: It's a lemon. It was nothing but a problem from day one. Or it's an orange. There were some problems with the car and it wasn't all that bad, but they wouldn't buy another one.

Reason #2: They're tired of it. They've had it five years now and are ready for a change.

Reason #3: They're upgrading/downgrading. "We're buying a brand new car." "My wife is pregnant and we need a 4-door sedan now." "I need to get a truck for my business." "All our kids have moved out, and I always wanted a sports car."

Reason #4: They're moving out of state, overseas, to another planet, etc.

Reason #5: They need money. "My wife is pregnant, and I have to sell my convertible." "We owe Uncle Sam big time this year."

Reason #6: They don't need/drive it anymore. "It was an extra car that has been sitting for a long time."

Reasons #3 through #6 are the ones I like to hear when I call about a car. Reason #2 can be okay, but whenever I hear it I become very wary that there's a hidden problem with the car. It's the most common reason people use when in fact the real reason is Reason #1. Of course, you won't ever hear anyone use Reason #1 and neither should you, unless you don't want to sell it. Whether you have a real lemon or just an orange on your hands, use Reason #2. After all, you're telling the truth. You *are* tired of it.

If your auto has had countless repairs, it's up to you to decide if you should offer that information to a potential buyer. One thing to consider, though; a car with countless repairs when there's only 60 or 80 thousand miles on it will look bad in the eyes of the buyer. They will think that the car hasn't been cared for properly or that it is problematic. You may just want to offer information on the big things that have been done, such as a new transmission, new clutch, new engine, etc. These may seem attractive to the buyer. They will think the car has a new life. And hopefully you saved your receipts and can back up what you say.

PREPPING YOUR CAR FOR SALE

Nothing can help sell a car quicker than a nice detail job. People get turned off real fast when they see a dirty car with a filthy interior and grimy engine compartment. Whether you're the kind of person who keeps his or her car spotless, or tends to let things go, now is the time to make that set of wheels sparkle. Is your engine running rough and in need of a tune-up? If it is, get it taken care of now. Tune-ups aren't that expensive.

The next step would be to fix all the little things you have been putting off that are inexpensive to replace. Broken window cranks, missing door lock knobs, frayed wiper blades, etc., things like these are nickle-and-dime stuff that can be easily replaced. You want to eliminate all the negatives on you car. In the case of something that costs a few bucks, like a broken tail-light lens, try calling around to the salvage yards. If you have a common car, chances are good that you will find the part you need and save yourself some dough by avoiding the cost of new.

Is your car running fine and all the little things have been fixed? If it is, then you are ready to start detailing. There are two ways you can go about this. You can pay someone else to do it or you can do it yourself.

THE LAZY PERSON'S WAY

If you have some extra money that you don't mind parting with, you could drop your car off at an auto detailing shop for a few hours. There they will steam clean your engine, wash and wax your car, and clean your upholstery and carpets all for about a $100, give or take. If your car's paint is faded from the sun, the auto detailer will buff out the paint with a polishing compound which will do wonders for your car's look. It's well worth the extra charge.

THE PERSON-WITH-A-LOT-OF-ENERGY WAY

If you're into saving money and have some extra time (and energy), you could easily do it yourself. You will want to arm yourself with some good cleaners for the vinyl, upholstery, and tires. As for the greasy engine compartment, take it to a detail shop just for the engine steam clean. You should be able to get this service for $25 or so and then you can do the rest of the cleaning yourself. The engine wash should be the first step in cleaning your car.

Give your car a good hand wash, including under the wheel wells and door jams. If your car has spent a lot of time in the sun, its paint will be faded. Get yourself some polishing compound and follow the directions. You'll want to rub it out before waxing it. And by the way, buffing out your car with polishing compound requires some elbow grease. You'll get a sore hand, but it's worth it in the end.

After washing and buffing out your car you'll want to wax it with a good brand of wax. And with your hand already sore from buffing it out, this would be a good time to recruit an assistant.

For tires, there are cleaners on the market now where you just spray it on and let it drip off. It doesn't get much easier than that. How are your rims/wheel covers? You'll want them to match the rest of the car, so get the appropriate cleaner and take care of them too.

For the interior, get out the vacuum cleaner and upholstery cleaner and window cleaner and go to it. A scrub brush will help you get any stains out of the seats. For dust in hard-to-get places like inside the air vents, use Q-tips. Don't forget the trunk and spare tire compartment. Clean! Clean! Clean! Once you have finished, your car will look so good you may decide not to sell it after all!

CALIFORNIA RESIDENTS ONLY

If you live in California, the Department of Motor Vehicles designates the seller as the responsible party for getting the car smogged. As I mentioned before, you can always negotiate this with the buyer if you really don't want to hassle with it. But keep in mind, you'll find that people will try to knock $50 or $100 off your asking price just for smog, even though it costs less than $30 for the inspection and certificate. Their alibi is there could be some adjustments or something in need of repair in order to get it to pass smog, which will cost more money.

Do yourself a favor; if you know that your car will pass smog with no problem, do it. The certificate is good for 90 days, which is more than enough time to sell your car. This way the buyer will have one less area to haggle with you when you show him the certificate.

ASKING PRICE

As described in the **Research** chapter of this book, you will be constantly scanning the ads to see what the market is getting for the type of car(s) you're after. So as long as you're already reading the ads, watch to see how much cars identical to yours are going for as well. This is the most accurate information you have that will tell what your car is worth.

Also in the **Research** chapter, you were to find out what the book price is of the car you are researching. As long as you're at it, find out what your own car is listed for. If your car is in primo condition with low miles then you should add to the price, just as the book states. But if your car has something major wrong with it, like a big dent, obviously it won't be worth as much as the price guide states. The general rule of thumb, however, when figuring how much to advertise your car for, is that it's always wise to start high. You can always come down, but you can't go back up.

As I described before, you want to pad your asking price in anticipation of negotiating. Always pad your price by about 20 percent for cars under $3,000; i.e., if you want $1,000 for your car, ask $1,200. If you want $2,000 for your car, ask $2,400, etc. For cars that you expect to sell for $3,000 or more, don't pad your price by more than $500 or you will get too far out of the market range and throw money away on ads.

ADVERTISING

Your car is running its best, it's all detailed and looking good, and you California residents had it smogged. You are ready to run your first ad. As I mentioned earlier in this book, there are plenty of places to advertise your car, so how do you decide which publication to start in? If there are any publications in your area that offer free classified advertising, like we have here in Southern California, then by all means take advantage. Unless there's some kind of emergency in your life and you are in a big hurry to sell, there's no need to grand slam every venue with an ad. This will guarantee you a big advertising bill when maybe only one ad would have worked fine.

Remember I said never be in a hurry to buy a car? The same goes for selling one, too. Never be in a hurry to sell a car. You will never get full market value for it. Sure, all of us would like to sell our cars within a few days, but sometimes it takes longer to find the right buyer. If you are anxious to sell, you certainly don't want to show it when a potential buyer is looking at your car. If they sense you are in dire need of money, they will low-ball you with an offer. So make like the poker player with a full house and be deadpan.

As for advertising, you can start by putting a "For Sale" sign in the window. Make sure you don't put it where it will cause a dangerous blind spot. The rear driver's-side passenger window would be a good place.

If you live in a local area where people post ads on bulletin boards around post offices, grocery, and hardware stores then take advantage and make up some posters. As long as it's free, why not? A nice color photo of your car attached to your ad will make it stand out from the rest.

For paid advertising, I always start in the local newspaper classifieds and suggest you do the same. Your local paper is probably the most popular publication in town and anyone who's looking for a car will certainly be scanning the ads for one. A week-long ad should be a good start.

In all advertising, the more lines you need the more you will be charged. Keeping it short and sweet will save you some money. The goal is to make it reach your target buyer(s) and be appealing at the same time.

You should start by including the year, make, and model. Include engine type i.e., 350, V6, 4-cyl, etc., only if your model offered more than one engine size. Mention whether it has an automatic transmission or 4-speed, 5-speed, etc. If your car offered either 2- or 4-door models, mention what yours is. If your car has low mileage then you definitely want to include it. If it has high miles, don't mention it. State any other key features that it may offer like convertible, four-wheel-drive, etc. Also, if your car has air-conditioning and you live in the south where air is highly desirable, mention it as well. Some people, myself included, can't live without AC.

If you are the original owner or the second owner, mention it. If you had some major work, like a rebuilt engine for which you have receipts, mention that too. You only have so much room in the ad and you can't include everything, so all that middle-of-the-road stuff you had done to your car can be described later over the phone. An ad stating new brakes or a new battery or a new clutch really won't sell your car any faster.

The ad's whole purpose is to attract the right person, and finding the right person will be easier when you list the key features of your car. For example, if you fail to mention that your car is a 5-speed, everyone interested in an automatic model will be calling to find out what yours is, wasting their time as well as yours.

As for all those frilly things like power windows, power this and that, and your fancy stereo, you can save it for your pitch over the phone or, if your car has them all, use one word - *loaded*.

Finally, one last descriptive word for the hook. You want to end your ad with something like *Dependable*, *Clean*, or *Garaged*. So a properly worded ad might go something like these:

> '79 Chevy Camaro. Rebuilt 350
> w/receipts, auto, loaded, runs xlnt,
> 2nd owner, clean. $2400 555-1234

> '84 Toyota Corolla. 4 dr, 5 spd, air,
> 95k. Dependable $2700 555-4321

Always abbreviate where you can. If you're not sure what to shorten, the ad consultant in the classified department who does this all day long can help you. Make sure you include your asking price; otherwise you will be plagued by callers wanting to know your price. Remember, dealers read the ads daily, always looking for a deal. Listing the price will screen them out along with the wishful thinkers.

THE PHONE CALLS

You need to prepare yourself for the kind of questions people will ask. If you were selling the '79 Camaro above, the first question I would ask, after confirming the information in print, is who rebuilt the engine? So have your receipts out and ready. I would also want to know how many miles are on the car and how many miles are on the rebuilt engine. If you are the second owner and all this work was done before you bought it, study that receipt. All this information should be on there.

Other questions I would ask are, "How long have you owned it? Who was the original owner? How often was the oil changed and who did the maintenance? Has it ever been in an accident" or "Are there any dents or scratches? Are all the power options working? Is anything broken or in need of repair?" If you've owned the car for some time, you should know all this off the top of your head. If you don't, find out. Know your car.

Always let callers ask the first round of questions. When they seem finished, offer the information about the middle-of-the road stuff like your new tires, new brakes, new battery, etc. If they seem interested and they haven't already asked, don't forget to mention the window dressings like all your power options and that fancy stereo.

In used car selling there are times to fib and times to be honest. Many people will probably ask you how long you've had it for sale and if anyone else has looked at it yet. No matter how long you've had it for sale or how many people have looked at it, the answer to these two questions is always the same. You have just put it up for sale and no one has seen it yet.

This makes people hungry to come over for a look. Deals don't last and if you tell them that three others have looked at it and it didn't sell, it tells the buyer that either there's something wrong with your car or you have it priced too high. But when no one else has looked at it, interest is stirred with thoughts of a deal ripe for the picking.

On the other hand, if your car has a major problem, such as rust or damage from an accident, don't lie and try luring people over without mentioning it over the phone. It's not like they won't notice. Be honest and up front with them; otherwise you will be causing hard feelings, wasting people's time and yours. There's nothing worse than driving a long way to look at a car that you never would have bothered with had you been properly informed in the first place.

THE APPOINTMENT

When you're selling a car, try to be accommodating and flexible when making the appointment. Everyone works, so weekends are most likely when you'll get people over. However, if someone wants to come over early on a weekday morning or on a weeknight, take the time to do it.

This is a sign of someone who needs a car right away, who will probably give you close to your asking price, if not all, providing he likes your car. If you push him off until the weekend he may find something else by then and you'll never hear from him again. So it may be well worth it to show up late for work or miss your game down at the ball field.

Before you give up time at work, it is wise to find out ahead that the caller is indeed a serious buyer and not just a browser. You will find that many people will call, act interested, tell you they're coming, and then never show. They either found another car and didn't have the decency to call and cancel or, for reasons that are beyond me, are afraid to say they are not interested and tell you they're coming anyway when they have no intention of doing so. This can be extremely frustrating when you are taking time out of your busy schedule to accommodate them.

The way to weed these people out is easy. Just ask them directly, "Are you really coming over? I don't want to take time off work for nothing." When they say yes, ask them to call back right before they are ready to come by and you will give them directions then. If you hear back from them, you can count on them coming by. If you don't hear from them, they would have been a no-show.

If someone calls and wants to come over now, ask for his phone number just in case something comes up and you need to reschedule. About fifteen minutes before he is supposed to arrive, call the number. If you get no answer or a recording with his name on it, then it looks like you have a serious buyer on his way over. If you get a wrong number, go to your ball game.

When the person shows up to look at your car, be friendly and greet him by his name (which you found out over the phone), shake his hand, and make eye contact. I know this sounds like something a used car salesman would do, but what the heck, at this point you *are* a used car salesman. Hang back and let the buyer look it over. Some people, you will find, are timid about looking at a car, so don't force information upon them. Make them feel comfortable. If they want to know something, they will ask.

While they are looking, you have a folder with all the related receipts and the title of ownership at your disposal. The current registration should already be in the car. Offer to show these if they would like. Also offer to open the hood and trunk. Timid lookers may be too shy to ask and because you spent so much time cleaning, you want to show off all the car's selling points.

When they want to take it for a test drive, go with them even if they have a passenger and you must sit in your cramped back seat. I'm always leery about letting strangers take off in my car. It's not that I'm so worried about them stealing it. I worry more about them getting into an accident. People not familiar with your neighborhood might run a stop sign, get lost, or mixed up. If you're there in the car you can direct them where to go. Have a route all picked out in advance. Just like I discussed in the **Test Drive** chapter, you want to direct them to a quiet street and to a freeway or the equivalent.

When you go with them on the test drive, there's nothing wrong with talking about the weather in a friendly way, but don't sit there talking nonstop about irrelevant topics. This is very annoying and the buyers may think you are trying to distract them from a hidden problem. Just sit back and leave the floor open. Let them ask the questions. If they bring up unrelated topics, then it's okay to partake.

After the test drive, the buyers may want to check under the hood again to look for oil leaks, etc. If anything is in question, offer to let them have their mechanic look it over--at their expense, of course. Sometimes people gain your trust and won't find it necessary. So all that is left to do is agree on a price. If they do prefer to have their mechanic look at it, try to be as flexible as possible.

NEGOTIATING

When it comes time to negotiate, the advice is pretty much the same as I outlined in the **Negotiation** chapter, except now the roles are reversed. The seller, whether he takes your car to a mechanic or not, will try to find things wrong with it to use as bargaining leverage to get you to lower your price. Fortunately, you have already padded your asking price in anticipation of this and are ready to come down some.

In settling on a price, there are some things to consider. Even though you have determined in your mind what your bottom price is, if you and the buyer have come to within $100 or $200 of meeting each other and he doesn't want to budge, you have to ask yourself these questions. Is my selling price realistic? Has my phone been ringing? Are there others interested in looking at it, or is this person the only one so far? Is there anything wrong with this car which the buyer is unaware of that makes it not worth as much?

If you haven't been getting much of a response from your ad, you may want to succumb to the buyer's offer. However, if your phone has been ringing off the hook, then hang tough and only give in a little. When you inform the buyer that you have had lots of calls, this will make him realize that if he wants your car, then he better act quickly with a sweeter offer.

Let's say you are selling your well-maintained car for $2,500. Except for being used, there really is nothing wrong with it. What do you do if someone comes over and low balls you with a $1,500 offer? Chances are the person is a dealer and trying to tempt you with cash. He will simply take the car and sell it off his lot, making at least $1,000 if not $1,500. So if this happens, hang tough and don't let him intimidate you. Just smile and say "Sorry." He might ask you what your bottom price is. If he does, tell him and stick to it no matter what.

Another tip in negotiating is don't advertise your bottom price followed by the word *firm*. Someone like me is going to offer a lower price anyway and, chances are, if your phone hasn't been ringing, you'll give in.

Always pad your price. There's something about negotiating that gives people a sense of accomplishment when you lower your price to meet them. In their eyes they just saved some money and this makes them feel good. When you advertise a *firm* price with the intention of not budging, people tend to make lower offers regardless. When you don't budge, they sometimes become too proud to give in to your full price. So you are forced to make a choice: you either go below your bottom price or lose the sale.

Also, don't let yourself get suckered by someone who wants your car, but won't have the money until either he sells his car or money comes in from some other unpredictable source. THE FIRST PERSON WHO COMES UP WITH THE CASH GETS YOUR CAR. If he wants to leave a deposit and have you hold the car until he gets his finances together, fine. Ask for a $100 non-refundable deposit and hold the car for no more than a week. You want to be sure he is serious about buying your car.

If by the end of the week he comes up empty, but still wants you to hold your car for him, get another $100 deposit. Should he default, you pocket the deposit for the inconvenience. In the meantime, write down all the numbers to callers who called on your ad so if the deal falls through, you can call them back.

When you go to transfer your vehicle, have all the paperwork in order. If you have lost your title, get a duplicate made up BEFORE you are ready to sell. In California it takes four to six weeks to get a duplicate title sent to you. It makes it easier to sell your vehicle when you have all the documents.

Even though it can be easily done, people are not always comfortable transferring a vehicle into their name without a title. Sometimes they will refuse until you have the title in your hands, so not having the title can sometimes cost you a sale. You can't blame them though. You may be on the up and up, but they don't know you from Adam. Without the title, they might think the car is stolen or has a lien against it. So have all your paperwork in order: title, registration, state inspections and, for us Californians, odometer disclosure and smog certificates.

A FEW LAST TIPS

•When a person buys a used car without a warranty, he is buying the car "as is". This means if he is driving it home on the day of the sale and the transmission blows up, he can't take it back to the seller for repair or his money back.

For your own protection, I recommend you write this out on the handwritten receipt. John Doe has purchased such-and-such vehicle "as is" on such-and-such day for such-and-such amount. Cars bought and sold between private parties are always assumed "as is", but writing it out on the receipt protects you in case someone comes back claiming you somehow misled them.

•If you're a single woman selling your car, it's not advisable to be alone when showing your car to strangers, especially while on the test drive. Arrange to have a friend with you. It's a sad society we live in today. You just can't trust people anymore.

•Never sell your car by setting up a payment plan where someone takes your car and pays you in monthly installments. YOU ARE NOT A BANK. Even if it's a trusted friend or relative, don't take the chance. Accidents do happen and cars do get stolen, and if he failed to get insurance you're out of a car. If he suddenly becomes unemployed and can't make the payments, you get to choose between being patient until he gets a new job, taking the loss, or becoming the ugly repossessor. Of course, by this time you and you're "trusted" friend or relative will no longer be speaking.

•In setting a price on your car, don't let the Blue Book sway you too much. It's just a price guide. The real world goes by supply and demand. But it is good to know the book price to use as a reference during negotiations. The best way to see what the market is on your car is by studying the classifieds for a month or so. To take this one step further, you could call the ads for cars identical to yours a week or two after they were published to find out if they sold and for how much.

THE NINE GOLDEN RULES TO SELLING YOUR CAR

1) Detail your car before selling it
2) Have all necessary titles, inspections, and paperwork in order
3) Know your car's market value
4) Publish effective ads
5) Separate the looky loos from the serious buyers over the phone
6) Be flexible when making the appointment
7) Negotiate, but don't give away your car just to get rid of it
8) No financing anyone, even friends or relatives.
9) Never be in a hurry to sell a used car

CHAPTER 9:

CAR CARE

Now that you have gone through all the trouble of finding a good used car, and paid a mechanic to check it over, TAKE CARE OF IT! Between the previous owner and the maintenance schedule in your owner's manual, find out immediately if the car needs service now and/or what it will be needing next. Anything that's due, get it taken care of pronto. The baby is now in your hands.

By taking care of your car, you're protecting your investment. Remember, the better shape it's in when it's your turn to sell, not only will you get top dollar for it, but it will be easier to sell as well. The following chapter offers car maintenance information, gasoline concerns, warm-up procedures, and some great car care tips which will enable you to enjoy many problem-free miles.

YOUR OWNER'S MANUAL

You most definitely want the owner's manual to your car. So if it has been lost, check with the dealer about getting a replacement for your model and year. If they're no longer available, try to get a manual for your model from a later year. If you strike out there, then you'll be forced to buy a repair manual for your car, which can be found at most auto parts stores.

If you like to tinker, obtaining a repair manual wouldn't be such a bad idea anyway. The repair manual offers much more insight on your car's maintenance and repairs for the do-it-yourselfer, with how-to chapters on everything from changing a fuse to a complete engine overhaul. The troubleshooting section alone is worth the price.

Do understand, though, that a repair manual would be a *supplement* to your owner's manual, not a substitute. Owner's manuals offer much more detailed information about your car, such as cold morning starts, when to shift the manual transmission, dash features, etc. So don't get a repair manual as a substitute when an owner's manual is available. However, when they're not available, a repair manual is better than no manual.

The maintenance schedules in both manuals will offer important information you need to know about when to adjust/replace the valves, idle speed, transmission fluid, air filter, spark plugs, timing, timing belt, etc. It all goes by mileage or time, whichever comes first.

Most owner's manuals offer two or more maintenance schedules to follow, depending on how you drive your car. There may be a "normal" driving maintenance schedule, a "unique" driving maintenance schedule, a "severe" driving maintenance schedule, and/or a "severe weather" driving maintenance schedule. The confusing thing about all this is what's considered normal driving in most owner's manuals isn't really normal at all.

How many of us never do any stop-and-go city driving or repeated short trips or experience dusty, rough or salt-laden roads or prolonged periods of freezing cold, heat, humidity or rain? That pretty much sums up all the climates in the United States, doesn't it?

Most owner's manuals consider "normal" driving to be without any of these elements, but is that possible? Don't let this fool you. You would have to live in a dry (but not dusty) climate that never gets hot or cold, where the roads are smooth and your driving is from point A to B with no stops in between, with trips being a minimum of 5 miles long, giving the engine sufficient warm up.

This certainly would be ideal for your car, but it's an unlikely reality. So forget the "normal" maintenance schedule in your owner's manual and go with the "severe" or "unique" schedule. You want the one that calls for more frequent servicing, which will help you keep your car in tip-top shape.

ABOUT OIL

I had mentioned earlier about the importance of regular oil changes. Let me stress this again. OIL SERVICE IS THE MOST IMPORTANT THING YOU CAN DO FOR YOUR CAR. When you read your owner's manual and it recommends oil changes every 5,000 miles, 7,500 miles, or even 10,000 miles, this is one section of your owner's manual I want you to ignore. Whether you change your own oil or you have it done at a lube center, CHANGE YOUR OIL AT LEAST EVERY 3,000 MILES OR 3 MONTHS, WHICHEVER COMES FIRST - NO IFS, ANDS, OR BUTS! Every 2,000 or 2,500 miles would be even better.

There have been many studies on the frequency of oil changes and its effect on engine parts. One thing always holds true: the more frequent the oil changes, the longer the engine will last. It doesn't matter if you own a Volkswagen or a Mercedes, you will get more miles and value out your car with frequent oil changes than someone who doesn't.

For example, a car that has had its oil changed every 3,000 miles may get more than 200,000 miles on the engine before there's a need for major repairs, whereas the same car that had its oil changed every 7,500 miles may not even make it to 100,000 miles before it needs engine work. God forbid if you change your oil every 10,000 miles!

Consider the facts. Oil is still cheap. If you change your oil every 3,000 miles, then in 200,000 miles you would have changed your oil 66 times. Let's say your car takes five quarts of oil. Multiply this times 66 equals 330 quarts. This, multiplied by $1.50 per quart equals $495. Now, using the same formula to figure how much you would spend on oil at intervals of 7,500 miles, I came up with $195--$300 dollars less. It doesn't make sense to save $300 in oil so you can run your $1,500 engine out of life twice as fast.

Clearly, frequent oil changes are the way to go. Even if your car has 90,000 miles on it and the previous owner changed the oil every 7,500 miles, don't think it's too late to do any good by increasing the oil changes now. It will. You truly slow down the engine's aging process with more frequent oil changes.

For those few of us who drive little, like less than 1,000 miles a month, make sure you change your oil every three months regardless. Even though you may have put as little as 1,500 miles on your car in this time span, the oil in your engine still breaks down with age and needs replacing. So low-mileage people, change oil by time intervals, not mileage, and you will be doing your car a big favor.

Now what grade of oil should you use? That information is in your owner's manual, or you can call your local dealership and ask them to look it up for you. Most likely it will be a 10W-30 or a 10W-40. Depends on where you live. As for what brand to use; everyone has their favorites. If you stick with a recognized name brand, you'll be fine. I don't recommend off-brands that you've never heard of. They may be okay and they may not. Why take a chance? OIL IS THE LIFE-BLOOD OF YOUR CAR!

And one last note about oil filters. CHANGE THE OIL FILTER EVERY TIME YOU CHANGE THE OIL. I've noticed some owner's manuals recommend that you change the filter every *other* time you change the oil. If this is what yours says, then ignore that part of your maintenance schedule as well. Again, oil filters are cheap. Why pour in five quarts of fresh oil only to have half a quart of filthy oil in the used filter that will pollute your new oil immediately? This doesn't make sense. Do your engine a big favor, change the filter every time and keep it clean in there.

If you were lucky and bought your car from someone who kept a maintenance record of all service and repairs, then you know exactly where you are with your car and when it's due for the next oil change. If the seller didn't keep records and doesn't know, or claims it was changed recently, but the oil looks dirty, get it changed pronto (honey-colored oil is fresh, while dark brown or black oil is old and due for a change).

OIL BURNERS

Most cars with more than a 100,000 miles on them will use oil. As a matter of fact, you can come to expect it from any car with an odometer reading in the six-figure range. This is not something to freak out about. As your engine wears, some oil will slip by the rings and burn off relatively clean. I'm not talking about cars billowing blue smoke behind them. That's another story. Cars that have high miles will usually use half to one-and-a-half quarts between a 3,000-mile oil change without any notice of smoke out your exhaust pipe. When you get up to two quarts, you'll be paying your mechanic's rent soon.

The key advice for proud owners in the six-figure odometer club is, not surprisingly, KEEP A CLOSE WATCH ON YOUR OIL LEVEL! Try not to let it get more than half a quart low. When you first get your car you should be checking the dipstick weekly. After a few months of close observation, you can gauge just how fast it's using oil either by mileage or time intervals. Use this for future reference to know when it's time to check/add the next half quart. The proper oil level will keep your motor purring like a content kitty for many more miles to come.

OTHER FLUID CONCERNS

If you bought a car with an automatic transmission from someone who didn't keep a maintenance record, ask when was the last time the transmission was serviced. If the previous owner doesn't know, get it done pronto. Ditto goes for manual transmission cars with upward of 100,000 miles on them. If the owner doesn't know when or if the gear oil has ever been changed, do it now. It's not that expensive. If your car has a differential (rear wheel drive), have this oil changed at the same time. After all, they work together and this is a good way to start out with a clean slate.

It's worth noting here that most manual transmissions require a heavy 90-weight gear oil, but not all do. Some of today's front-wheel-drive transaxles require a much thinner 30-weight oil. If-90 weight is mistakenly used, gears can burn up by not receiving the proper lubrication, resulting in costly repairs. As you can imagine, a simple mix-up like this could easily happen at a quick lube center where some inexperienced or uninformed attendant is changing your oil. MAKE SURE YOU KNOW WHAT WEIGHT OIL GOES IN YOUR TRANSMISSION, AND RELAY THAT INFORMATION TO THE ATTENDANT WHO CHANGES IT!

As for the rest of the car's maintenance, you will have to work from the evidence you have. Aside from the oil and transmission fluid, make sure you check all the other fluids: brake, power steering (if your car has it), hydraulic clutch (if your car has it), battery water level (if it's not maintenance free), windshield washer fluid, and the coolant level.

When the engine is cold, look inside your radiator to see what color the fluid is. It should be a greenish yellow color. If yours is anything but that, have your cooling system flushed and new coolant added. If it is yellowish green, you will be okay for now. Make a note to check it during your next oil change. Most cars today offer a reservoir tank for the coolant with a high and low mark in which to keep the fluid between. You can find the tank by locating the small hose that comes from under the radiator cap and following it to the unit.

Periodically check the coolant level and make sure you keep it between those marks. Follow directions according to your owner's manual and mix the correct ratio of coolant and water. Always use distilled water for your cooling system and for batteries that are not maintenance free. Water from your tap may have high concentrations of minerals which could corrode the inside of your radiator or harm the cells in your battery.

LUBE CENTERS

Quick lube service stations make life easy for car owners who don't have the time or know-how for car maintenance. For about 20 bucks you're in and out in 10 minutes with a fresh oil change. You don't even get out of your car! When you first buy your car, I recommend paying extra for the deluxe service where they do a fourteen-point check service. Not only do they change your oil, they also check fourteen points on your car, topping off all fluids. Some will even vacuum and wash your windows!

When it's all said and done, the attendant will inform you of any fluids that were low, anything that may be leaking, if your coolant needs a flush, if an air cleaner is in need of replacement, or any other service that may need immediate attention or be just around the corner. For those who don't know much about cars, quick lube service centers are a time and money saver. And remember to save your receipts! Check the yellow pages under service stations for quick lube centers in your area.

TIRES

Get into the habit of periodically checking your tires' air pressure. Too much or too little air can cause your tires to wear prematurely. You can pick up a pressure gauge at any auto parts store for a couple of bucks and keep it in your glove box where it's handy. Air pressure should be checked when the tires are cold or you may get a biased reading. A short trip to your local service station won't matter, but a half-hour trip on a hot day could.

When you are checking air pressure, also check the tires' tread for uneven wear. If you have been good about keeping the right amount of air pressure and start to notice uneven wear, it usually means you have developed an alignment problem. Let it go, and you will also be paying for new front tires along with your front-end alignment. Early detection will allow you to save your existing tires and some cash.

Also, a good way to squeeze a few extra thousand more miles out of your tires is by having them rotated regularly. Most tire centers will rotate your tires for free, provided the tires are the brand they sell. Even if you didn't purchase the tires yourself, contact the tire store that sells the brand tires that are on your car and ask to have them rotated. Most tire shops won't require a receipt. Get your tires rotated every 10,000 miles.

ENGINE PING AND GASOLINE

If you notice your engine has started knocking it could be a couple of things. Your engine may be a few degrees out of time, indicating the need for a tune-up. Or, if it is a manual transmission, you may be driving in the wrong gear and lugging the engine, which is a no-no (manual transmission people, make sure you are in the right gear). However, if you're not due for a tune-up, the most likely reason for engine knock is poor-quality gas from your last fill-up. Engine run-on, where your car wants to keep running after it is turned off, is also a symptom.

Not all gasolines are created equal. An 87 octane rating at one station may not be the same as the 87 rating at another, and the same goes for the higher octane ratings as well. It gets involved, but the octane rating posted at the pumps is reached by adding together the ratio of the Research Octane Number and the Motor Octane Number and then dividing it in two. Because these ratios can vary without affecting the posted octane rating, the gas at one station may be much better quality than the gas at another.

Good advice here would be to avoid the el cheapo gas stations and stick with the nationally known chains. You will pay a few cents more at the pump, but you get more than that back through better mileage and an engine that will run smoother and last longer.

So before you pay to have your car tuned up because it's been pinging, suspect poor quality gas and do some experimenting. Start by trying the 87 octane rating at several reputable stations. If this doesn't clear up the knocking, bump up to the 89 octane rating and start over. Sooner or later you will fill up with a tank of gas that has cleared up your engine ping and Eureka! You have found your gas station. Stick with them. And it would be safe to assume that if the

89 octane rated gas at station X down the street that cleared up the knocking, then the 89 octane gas at station X across town or across the country, for that matter, will have the same effect.

Just as gasoline is different, so are cars. Some cars are more sensitive to the quality of gas, while others run fine and dandy on the cheapest gas in town. Usually this becomes evident when you have made a change in vehicle ownership. As described above, do some experimenting.

For fuel-injected cars, a quality grade of gas is imperative. Engines with fuel injectors usually require a higher rated octane than carbureted ones. Check your owner's manual for recommendations or call your car's respective dealer and ask the service department what they suggest.

TUNE-UP

As your owner's manual will show, regular tune-ups are a good form of preventive maintenance. Periodically, all cars need them to continue running their best. Because the change in your engine is very gradual and most owner's manuals call for a tune-up before the engine has had a chance to sound bad, the need for a tune-up is usually not noticeable. This is the time to forget the "if it ain't broke don't fix it" rule. Get your car tuned when it's due.

A minor tune-up, or minor service as it's now called, is usually every 30,000 miles. It would include the following: new oil and oil filter, air cleaner, spark plugs, fuel filter, coolant flush, chassis lubrication, valve adjustment, and idle speed adjustment for carbureted engines. Inspection of drive belts, fuel lines, steering linkage, brake system, exhaust system, cooling system, and all fluid levels should be performed as well. Some cars will also have their manual/automatic transmission fluids changed at this time, while others may be on their own schedule. This should clear up any hard starting or rough idle problems.

A major tune-up, or major service, which is usually every 60,000 miles, would include all of the above with the addition of a new timing belt (if your car has one), fuel filter, EGR valve, PVC valve; replacement of worn belts and hoses may be necessary as well. Keep in mind that all cars' tune-up intervals vary. Go by what your owner's manual says.

REPAIR FRAUD

The best way to avoid automotive repair fraud is to always insist on a written estimate (in many states, this is the law). Request that any changes in the estimate can only be made with your approval, and ask that the old parts be saved for your inspection.

If you ever pay for automotive work that wasn't done correctly, or feel you have been sold unnecessary parts or service, California has the Bureau of Automotive Repairs to help address these problems. They require you to file a complaint form along with copies of your receipts for the work done. You will then be assigned a representative who will mediate between you and the repair shop for either new work or a refund, depending on the situation.

The Bureau also offers *A Consumer's Guide to Automotive Repair,* which is a free brochure that tells you how to select a good mechanic, outlines your rights as a consumer, and shows you how to file a complaint. You can obtain a complaint form or the brochure by calling 800-952-5210. If you don't live in California, start by contacting your state's Consumer Protection Agency. If they can't help, they should know who can.

ENGINE WARM-UP

There has been much confusion lately about the proper way to warm up your car. Actually it boils down to two conflicting opinions--the old rule of thumb and the new rule of thumb.

The old rule of thumb was to warm up your car before driving it, especially in the morning. The colder the temperature outside, the longer you would need to warm it up. In the summer 60 seconds may be sufficient, while in the frigid winter it may take 4 or 5 minutes. Also, when first driving off, you should take it easy on the gas pedal until the car reaches normal operating temperature.

The theory behind the old rule of thumb is that when your car sits, all the oil ends up in the pan. When you start your engine in the morning, it takes a minute or two for the oil to warm up and circulate throughout. Starting your cold engine and driving off without first warming it up would put extra wear on moving parts before the oil has sufficiently coated the insides. With the first minute or so of metal against metal, day after day after day, people who didn't warm up their cars supposedly found themselves paying for repairs much sooner than the those who religiously did their warm-ups. Makes sense, right? Fasten your seat belts.

The new rule of thumb is to let your engine warm up only 10 to 20 seconds and drive off slowly, taking it easy on the accelerator until the engine is up to normal operating temperature. In frigid temperatures, a few more seconds of idling may be necessary before driving off.

The theory behind the new rule of thumb is that because most engine wear occurs when the engine is cold, the sooner you warm up to normal operating temperature, the sooner there won't be cold engine wear. An engine warms quicker when it is being driven rather than when it's sitting there idling for a minute or two.

Both opinions agree that most engine wear occurs between the time it is first started and the time it reaches normal operating temperature. This usually requires 5 to 10 miles of driving, depending on the outside temperature and how long ago the engine was last run.

Both opinions also agree that driving during the warm-up process should be taken slow and easy until the engine has reached normal operating temperature. Slow and easy means being very gentle on the accelerator to gradually increase your speed and to barely go the speed limit. No hard accelerations or revving the engine when it's cold.

So which warm-up method should you practice? It appears that the old rule of thumb may apply to older engines, while the new rule of thumb may apply to today's sophisticated motors. To be certain which category your car falls under, check your owner's manual and follow what it says about warming up the car, or call your car's respective dealership and ask the service department their opinion. Whichever warm-up method you use, the most important step is driving slow and easy until the car has reached normal operating temperature.

CAR CARE TIPS

•Whenever you drive your car it's a good idea to take it easy all the time, not just during the warm-up process. When people take it easy on their cars, their cars return the favor and take it easy on their pocketbook. When you constantly accelerate hard and brake hard, you shorten the life of all related parts--namely the engine, transmission, clutch, and brakes. Get the picture? So get into the habit of taking it easy. Your car will love you for it.

•Previous owners who kept records and all their receipts make life easy for those of us who buy their cars. Regardless of what your previous owner did, this is what you need to do. Every time you change the oil, write down the mileage and the date and the grade of oil and type of filter you use. Every time you buy tires, replace the brakes, change the spark plugs, etc., log it down and keep those receipts!

If you have a computer you can open a new file and keep everything organized. If you don't, keep a file in your desk drawer for all those receipts and start a ledger for the oil changes. It will be easier to sell your car when a potential buyer has proof that the car has been well cared for. The next owner will appreciate it.

•If you're like me and like to tinker under the hood, but hate to get grease under your fingernails, go to your local drug store and by a box of surgical gloves. They are thin and tough and when you are through with surgery just peel them off and you still have clean fingernails and are now ready for your hot date.

•You may think I'm crazy with this one, but the best way I have found to keep battery terminals from corroding is by coating them with imitation maple syrup right before you go for a drive. The heat will cause the syrup to crystalize into a hard glass. If you need to give someone a jump-start you can easily break it off with the jumper cables. Recoat at your earliest convenience.

•The best way to detect leaks is by putting a flat piece of cardboard under your car. The next day you can pinpoint where the leak is coming from by the location of drops and the type of fluid found on the cardboard.

•As a safety measure, most cars with a manual transmission won't start unless you push in the clutch pedal first. That way, if the car is in gear and you try to start it, there's no danger of it lunging forward. If your car doesn't have this feature, get in the habit of doing it anyway. Not only is it a safe practice, it also saves on your battery and starter motor.

•If you do most of your own auto maintenance, watch for sales on oil, filters, etc., from your local auto parts store and stock up when the opportunity arises. Then when your car is due for an oil change, there's no running around trying to find the best price on oil and filters, etc.

•Contrary to the common method of warming up your engine before an oil change, I do just the opposite. Warming up the engine puts a fresh coating of oil on all the internal parts of your engine as well as some in your oil filter. However, a cold engine has all the oil in the pan and the oil filter is mostly drained. Because the cold oil is already in the pan, it really doesn't take any longer to drain out and you won't get messy oil dripping out of the oil filter when you change it.

•When searching for a place to park in a parking lot, get in the habit of picking a spot away from the crowd. This will greatly reduce the risk of someone tagging your car door. Besides, unless you are an aerobics trainer or professional sports star, we all could use a little more exercise in our lives.

•Along with parking away from the crowd is searching for a shady parking spot. This will save your dash, upholstery, and keep your paint from fading as well as keeping the inside of your car from becoming an oven. Also, leaving your windows cracked a half-inch will help alleviate the baking effect.

•Manual transmission people, when parking your car, get in the habit of setting your emergency brake before putting it in gear. This leaves the tension off your gear box and on your brakes where it belongs.

•Make sure all your dash gauges and lights are working properly and you understand what they mean. Temperature gauge, oil pressure gauge, battery gauge--if one of these light up while you're driving, you better know what to do or you may burn up your engine. You can find this information in your owner's manual or call your car's respective dealership and ask the service department to explain them.

•Once you have owned your car for a while you will become familiar with its sound. Always listen for any changes to that sound. Your car may send some early signals of repairs that are just around the corner. Even if it requires going to your mechanic, follow up on any unfamiliar noises and find out what's causing them, pronto. Early detection of a necessary repair can save dollars by getting it taken care of before other related parts become damaged.

•Do-it-yourselfers who change your own oil, make sure you discard your old oil properly. No pouring it back into the ground where it came from or throwing it in the trash where it will end up in the ground somewhere else. Used motor oil is highly toxic to our ground water. Save the used motor oil in jugs and periodically dispose of it at a recycling center that accepts it. Check with your city's public works department or with the service stations in your area. Some service stations accept used motor oil.

•Standard drivers, proper downshifting can make your car's brakes last many thousands of miles longer while the extra wear to your clutch is practically non-existent. Look in your owner's manual for proper downshifting methods for your car and get into the habit.

•If you live in a rainy climate you may need to have your chassis lubed more often than stated in your owner's manual. Constant splashing of water on the underside of your car can wash away grease and replace it with dirt. Suspension and steering linkage is expensive to replace.

•Get in the habit of gauging your gas mileage and know your average miles per gallon. Should that average begin to drop, it's a sign for a tune-up...or you may have caught some other minor repair before it becomes an expensive one.

•With many bumpers painted or plastic these days, you can't remove an unwanted bumper sticker using a razor blade without scratching it up good. Try using a hair blow dryer or squirt on some WD-40 and let it soak. Either of these will usually do the trick. WD-40 is also great for unwanted window decals.

•California residents, save all your old emission test reports. With results every two years revealing how many parts-per-million of hydrcarbons your car is emitting, this is valid evidence of how well you kept your car in tune, which is nice to show to potential buyers in the future.

•When in need of interior parts or body parts, consider the salvage yard. Things like a new bumper, tail-light lens, door panel, or front seat can be very expensive when bought new through a dealer. But at the salvage yard, you can get them for a fraction of the cost and they may be just as good as new. Make the auto graveyard your first call.

•If you notice bird poop on your car or someone eggs you on Halloween, get it washed off as soon as possible. Bird poop and eggs have acid in them that will eat away at your paint and permanently scar it.

THE SEVEN GOLDEN RULES OF CAR CARE

1) Read and understand your owner's manual completely
2) Have your oil changed at least every 3,000 miles or three months, whichever comes first
3) Have your car tuned up as required
4) Become accustomed to your car's sound and listen for changes in that sound.
5) Be aware of repair fraud
6) No hard driving on cold engines
7) Always keep records of all service and repairs performed on your car

APPENDICES

Appendix A:

The Used Car Buyer's Manual Directory of Reliable Used Cars

Italics denotes **Best Used Car Bets**

Acura Integra '86-'95
Acura Legend '86-'95
BMW 3-Series '85-'95
BMW 5-Series '85-'95
BMW 7-Series '85-'95
Buick Century '86-'95
Buick Electra V6 '85-'90
Buick Le Sabre (3.8 L) '85-'95
Buick Park Avenue V6 '91-'95
Buick Regal '84-'95
Cadillac De Ville '80-'95
Cadillac Eldorado '80-'95
Cadillac Fleetwood '80-'95
Cadillac Seville '80-'95
Chevrolet Camaro '80-'95
Chevrolet Caprice '80-'95
Chevrolet Cavalier '84-'95
Chevrolet Celebrity V6 '82-'91
Chevrolet Corvette '80-'95
Chevrolet Lumina '90-'95
Chevrolet Nova '85-'88
Chrysler Le Baron GTS '85-'88
Chrysler New Yorker (4cyl) '83-'88
Dodge Aries '84-'89
Dodge Caravan '84-'95
Dodge Challenger '80-'83
Dodge Colt '80-'94
Dodge Omni '80-'90
Dodge Ram 50 Trucks '83-'93
Dodge Spirit (except turbo) '89-'94
Ford Crown Victoria '82-'95

Ford Explorer '91-'95
Ford Festiva '88-'93
Ford Mustang V6 '83-'86
Ford Probe '89-'95
Ford Taurus V6 '88-'95
Ford Thunderbird (except 4cyl) '83-'95
Geo Metro '89-'95
Geo Prizm '89-'95
Geo Storm '90-'93
Geo Tracker '89-'95
Honda Accord '80-'95
Honda Civic '80-'95
Honda Prelude '80-'95
Infiniti G20 '91-'95
Infiniti J30 '93-'95
Infiniti M30 '90-'92
Infiniti Q45 '90-'95
Isuzu Trooper '91-'95
Isuzu Trucks '84-'94
Lexus ES250 '90-'91
Lexus ES300 '92-'95
Lexus LS400 '90-'95
Lexus SC300 '92-'95
Lexus SC400 '92-'95
Lincoln Continental '80-'95
Lincoln Mark VI '80-'83
Lincoln Mark VII '84-'92
Lincoln Mark VIII '93-'95
Lincoln Town Car '81-'95
Mazda 323 '86-'94
Mazda 626 '80-'95
Mazda 929 '88-'95

Mazda GLC '80-'85
Mazda Miata '90-'95
Mazda MVP '89-'95
Mazda MX-6 '88-'95
Mazda Protege '90-'95
Mazda RX-7 '80-'95
Mazda Trucks '80-'95
Mercedes-Benz 190E '84-'93
Mercedes-Benz 280E, CE/SE '78-'81
Mercedes-Benz 380SE, SL '81-'85
Mercedes-Benz 450SL '78-'80
Mercury Capri '80-'86 & '91-'94
Mercury Cougar (except 4cyl turbo XR-7) '84-'95
Mercury Grand Marquis '83-'94
Mercury Sable '88-'95
Mercury Tracer '88-'95
Mitsubishi Diamante '92-95
Mitsubishi Eclipse '90-'95
Mitsubishi Galant '85-'95
Mitsubishi Mirage '85-'95
Mitsubishi Montero V6 '89-'95
Mitsubishi Trucks '83-'95
Nissan Altima '93-'95
Nissan (Datsun) Trucks '80-'95
Nissan 200SX '80-'88
Nissan 240SX '89-'95
Nissan 300ZX '84-'95
Nissan Maxima '81-'95
Nissan Pathfinder '87-'95
Nissan Pulsar NX '83-'90
Nissan Sentra '82-'95
Nissan Stanza '82-'92
Oldsmobile Ciera '82-'95
Oldsmobile Cutlass & Cutlass Supreme '80-'95
Oldsmobile Delta 88 & Eighty Eight '80-'95
Oldsmobile Ninety Eight '80-'95
Plymouth Acclaim '89-'95
Plymouth Colt '83-'94

Plymouth Horizon '80-'90
Plymouth Laser '90-'94
Plymouth Reliant '86-'89
Plymouth Sundance '87-'94
Plymouth Voyager '84-'95
Pontiac 6000 '86-'92
Pontiac Bonneville '80-'95
Pontiac Firebird '80-'95
Pontiac Sunbird '86-'93
Saab 900 '80-'95
Saab 9000 Turbo '86-'95
Saturn SL, SC, & SW '91-'95
Subaru Justy '87-'94
Subaru Legacy '90-'95
Subaru Loyale '90-'94
Subaru Sedan '80-'89
Subaru SVX '92-'95
Subaru XT '85-'91
Toyota 4Runner '84-'95
Toyota Camry '83-'95
Toyota Celica '80-'95
Toyota Corolla '80-'95
Toyota Cressida '80-'92
Toyota Land Cruiser '80-'95
Toyota MR2 '85-'89
Toyota Previa '91-'95
Toyota Supra '86-'95
Toyota Tercel '84-'95
Toyota Trucks '80-'95
Toyota Van '84-'89
Volkswagen Cabriolet '85-'93
Volkswagen Golf '85-'95
Volkswagen Jetta '81-'95
Volvo 240 '87-'93
Volvo 740 '85-'92
Volvo 760 '83-'90
Volvo 940 '91-'95

Appendix B:
Inspection Checklist

Part One: Visual Inspection

	OK?	Cost to Repair/Replace - Notes
1) Body Damage - Accident		
Check for over spray		
Check for mismatched paint		
Eyeball body and seams		
2) Body Damage - Rust		
Check wheel wells/fenders		
Check flooring		
Check trunk		
Tap and listen to areas in question		
Rust repair? Method used		
3) Tires and Suspension		
All tires match?		
Tread depth?		
Test shock absorbers		
Does car sit level on flat surface?		

4) Fluids
Check oil - clean? dirty? full? low?
Check under oil filler cap
Auto transmission fluid - color? smell?
Coolant - color? reservoir level?
Inspect radiator/AC fins for damage

5) Air Filter - Clean? Dirty?

6) Check All Hoses

7) Check Drive Belts

8) Fluid Leaks
Oil seepage - oil pan? valve cover?
Check underside for: Oil?
Transmission fluid?
Coolant?
Brake fluid?

9) California Emissions
Check sticker - underside of hood
Check gas filler tube

10) Check Tailpipe
Color? light gray/brown is normal

	OK?	Cost to Repair/Replace - Notes
11) Glass		
Cracks or chips?		
12) Sunroof		
Factory or custom?		
Check full range of movement		
13) Interior - Check:		
Front seats		
Rear seats		
Head liner		
Carpeting		
Dash		
Odometer reading		
Glove box		
Windows - crank-up/electric		
Locks - power/manual - use key		
Heater		
Air conditioning		
Emergency brakes		
Horn		
Head lights - low/high beams		
Dome lights		

Dash lights	
Windshield washer/wipers	
Stereo	
Convertible tops - open & close	
Tilt steering	
Other power options	

14) Luggage Compartment

Opens with ignition key and remote?	
Spare tire?	
Jack?	
Lug wrench?	

Part Two: The Test Drive

1) Listen to Engine	OK?	Cost to Repair/Replace - Notes
Cold idle		
Odd sounds? - valves?		
Lifters?		
Exhaust leak?		
Undetermined		

2) Check brakes
Solid pedal?
Brakes evenly? - pulls to one side?
Brake noises - squeaks? grinds?

3) Check Alignment
Car drives straight or wanders
Steering wheel shimmy?

4) Check Transmission
Check reverse - noises?
Manual - shifts through gears easily?
Stick shift pops out of any gear?
Automatic shifts smoothly?

5) The Open Road
Car's performance at 50 mph
Check alignment again
When finished, check again for leaks

6) Check Receipts
Receipts for - repairs? new parts?
Maintenance records?
Odometer in accordance with receipts?

7) Seller's Character

Car's appearance?

Home and yard appearance?

8) At Your Mechanic

Highlight all items above in question

9) Check Recall Information

Recall Hotline #1-800-424-9393 or call

the respective dealership with the VIN

Additional Notes

-Order Form-

Use this form to order additional copies of *The Used Car Buyer's Manual.*

Quantity	Price	Total
CA residents: Add .72¢ sales tax per book.	+	
Shipping & Handling	+	
Total	$	

Discounts: Order three or more books and take 10% off the price. Yes! Buy three or more books and you pay only $8.95 each!

Shipping & handling: Add $2.50 for the first book and .75¢ for each additional book. Send check or Money Order to:

Pyramid West Publishing
P.O. box 830
Newbury Park, CA 91319

Closing Note

The publisher wishes to invite your criticisms about this book. Feel free to inform us of any mistakes, oversights, unclear subject matter, or any important points that we had missed. Your suggestions will be considered for future editions. Also, we would enjoy hearing your success stories that resulted from this manual. To reach us, write to the following address:

Pyramid West Publishing
P.O. Box 830
Newbury Park, CA 91319